Timing is Everything; Astrology is the Key

Book 2

By Weslynn McCallister

Writing as Wes Alistair

BALBOA.
PRESS
A DIVISION OF HAY HOUSE

This book has been previously published under the title of *Timing is Everything: Astrology is the Key. It has been re-edited and contains additional information.*

ISBN: 978-1-4525-5230-9 (sc)
ISBN: 978-1-4525-5231-6 (e)

Balboa Press books may be ordered through booksellers or by contacting:

Balboa Press
A Division of Hay House
1663 Liberty Drive
Bloomington, IN 47403
www.balboapress.com
1-(877) 407-4847

Because of the dynamic nature of the Internet, any web addresses or links contained in this book may have changed since publication and may no longer be valid. The views expressed in this work are solely those of the author and do not necessarily reflect the views of the publisher, and the publisher hereby disclaims any responsibility for them.

The author of this book does not dispense medical advice or prescribe the use of any technique as a form of treatment for physical, emotional, or medical problems without the advice of a physician, either directly or indirectly. The intent of the author is only to offer information of a general nature to help you in your quest for emotional and spiritual well-being. In the event you use any of the information in this book for yourself, which is your constitutional right, the author and the publisher assume no responsibility for your actions.

Any people depicted in stock imagery provided by Thinkstock are models, and such images are being used for illustrative purposes only.
Certain stock imagery © Thinkstock.

Printed in the United States of America

Balboa Press rev. date: 07/05/12

Also by Weslynn McCallister

Romance Novels

Apache Springs
Wyatt's Deck
Prophecies of the Ancients

Metaphysical Books by Weslynn McCallister, writing as Wes
Alistair
Romancing the Zodiac-Book Two

Poetry Book by Weslynn McCallister
Shifting Sands

Romantic Suspense Novels by Weslynn McCallister, writing as
Jamie Cortland
Skin Deep
Never Trust a Stranger

Contents

List Of Tables

WESTERN ASTROLOGY GLYPHS

Signs

Sign	Glyph
Aries	♈
Taurus	♉
Gemini	♊
Cancer	♋
Leo	♌
Virgo	♍
Libra	♎
Scorpio	♏
Sagittarius	♐
Capricorn	♑
Aquarius	♒
Pisces	♓

Planets

Planet	Glyph
Earth	⊕
Sol	☉
Luna	☽
Mercury	☿
Venus	♀
Mars	♂
Jupiter	♃
Saturn	♄
Uranus	♅
Neptune	♆
Pluto	♇ / ♇

Aspects

Aspect	Glyph
Conjunction	☌
Opposition	☍
Trine	△
Sextile	✶
Square	□
Quincunx	⚻
Semisquare	∟
Sesquiquadrate / sesquisquare	⊡
Semisextile	⚺
Quintile	Q
Biquintile	bQ

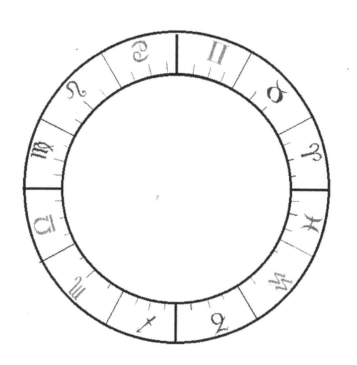

Part 1

Introduction

WHAT IS A HOROSCOPE?
HOW DOES IT WORK?

THE HOROSCOPE, or birth chart is virtually a snapshot of the heavens and their relationship to Earth at the exact time and place of your birth. At the moment you inhaled your first breath, you inhaled the planets electromagnetic energies. No one else on this Earth is or ever has been exactly like you. In the few instances that souls are born at the exact time and place, they are said to be twin souls. Though their lives are similar, free will has been bestowed upon all of us by God.

The Zodiac

The zodiac is determined by the vernal equinox, the position of the Sun on or near March 20 when the days and nights are equal in length. It begins at zero degrees of Aries which marks the beginning of the tropical zodiac, most often used in Western astrology. The natural order of the zodiac is: Aries, Taurus, Gemini, Cancer, Leo, Virgo, Libra, Scorpio, Sagittarius, Capricorn, Aquarius, and Pisces.

How Does Astrology Work?

Using the equal house system, the zodiac is divided into twelve signs of thirty degrees each, representing both the positive and negative characteristics of behavior and development. The effects on each area of our lives are determined by the positions of the planets and their interactions between the signs, houses and planets of our natal and progressed horoscopes. Daily transits of the planets through our natal horoscope indicate trends and challenges that will soon present themselves by their planetary vibrations. By carefully observing these trends, you will find the most advantageous days for every aspect of your life.

Chapter 1

THE ZODIAC

The zodiac is divided into twelve parts of a 360 degree circle. Using equal house astrology, each house is divided into thirty degrees each. Because of the revolution of the Earth around the Sun, it would appear that the Sun travels through the zodiac at the rate of one sign per month. Naturally, this causes our seasonal changes and astrologically speaking, it also modifies characteristics of those born during that time.

The signs are divided into four triplicities of three signs each that represent four specific temperaments. They are as follows:

The Fire Triplicity: Aries, Leo, Sagittarius – an impulsive nature, disposition to sudden illness, political and speculative interests

The Earth Triplicity: Taurus, Virgo, Capricorn – artistic, imaginative, studious tendencies; a disposition to chronic disorders.

The Air Triplicity: Gemini, Libra, Aquarius- cheerful, social signs with a tendency to become over-exhausted.

The Water Triplicity: Cancer, Scorpio, Pisces-emotional and contemplative in nature.

The signs of the zodiac are also divided into three groups of quarters representing cardinal, fixed and mutable signs. They are as follows:

The cardinal signs which are capable of adjusting to circumstances and represent the change of seasons are:

Aries- representing the East and Spring
Cancer-representing the North and Summer
Libra-representing the West and Fall
Capricorn-representing the South and Winter.

The fixed signs that fall after the change of seasons and are set in their ways are: Taurus, Leo, Scorpio, and Aquarius.

The mutable signs that are able to adapt to circumstances easily are Gemini, Virgo, Sagittarius and Pisces. These signs fall at the end of the seasons.

QUESTIONNAIRE

Includes material from the Introduction and Chapter 1
The answers to all questions are found in the preceding chapters.

1. What is a horoscope?

2. Name the signs of the zodiac in their natural order.

3. How does Astrology work?

4. What signs are included within the Fire Triplicity?

5. Describe the nature of the Fire triplicity signs.

6. What signs are included in the Earth triplicity?

7. Describe the nature of the Earth triplicity signs.

8. What signs are included in the Water triplicity?

9. Describe the nature of the Water triplicity signs.

10. Name the Cardinal signs.

11. What sign represents the spring and the East?

12. Name the fixed signs.

13. Do these signs adapt easily to circumstances?

14. What are the mutable signs?

15. Do they fall at the beginning or at the end of the seasons?

Chapter 2

THE SIGNS OF THE ZODIAC

ARIES

March 21- April 19
Ruler: Mars
Fire Triplicity
Cardinal sign
Northern sign
Barren sign
Masculine sign
Negative sign
Equinoctial sign
Sign of short ascension, often found intercepted in horoscopes
Planet in exaltation in Aries: The Sun
Planet in detriment in Aries: Venus
Planet in its fall in Aries: Saturn
Archangel: Malchidial
Angel: Sharhiel

Aries is the first sign of the zodiac. He is spring, bursting out all over! Energetic, courageous and sometimes fool hardy, Aries goes where angels fear to tread. He is the innovator, the courageous one. He loves competition and charges ahead aggressively. Ambitious and enterprising, he is the pioneer.

Don't expect diplomacy from an Aries. He is independent, headstrong, excitable, and can be belligerent. He often suffers from headaches, migraines, and anxiety, He needs peaceful surroundings and plenty of rest. He should avoid caffeine and stimulants. His diet should be comprised mainly of vegetables and seafood.

In love, Aries is attracted to the fire and air signs of Gemini, Leo, Libra, Sagittarius and Aquarius.

First of the fire signs, ruled by Mars, his symbol is the ram. He is a cardinal sign, versatile and adaptable. You may find him among the athletes, carpenters, dentists, firefighters, police officers and surgeons.

Suggested herbs for Aries:

birch-The essential oil relieves muscle and headache pain and reduces fever. Do not use during pregnancy. Keep out of the reach of children.

chamomile-Avoid use during the first trimester of pregnancy. (Do not use blue chamomile. It is a variety of mugwort and must never be used during pregnancy.) This herb calms anger, nervous tension and anxiety, common to Aries.

eucalyptus-This respiratory oil is excellent not only for muscle aches, but also for burns. It may also be used as an insect repellant for mosquitoes. Use in moderation on the skin and avoid if you have a history of epilepsy. If hypertension is present, use with caution.

frankincense-may be used for scars, nervous tension, and as an anti-inflammatory. Avoid using in the first trimester of pregnancy and use in moderation in later stages of pregnancy.

ginger-may be used for nervous exhaustion, mental fatigue and to relieve fevers. Use in moderation on sensitive skin.

lavender-may be used to calm and restore emotional imbalance. It is excellent for burns, wounds cuts, headache and muscular pain. Do not use in first trimester of pregnancy.

lemon-may be used for anxiety, stress and fevers.

marjoram-may be used to relieve migraine headaches and muscle pain.

Questionnaire

1. What planet is the ruler of Aries?

2. What type of sign is Aries?

    a.   Fire
    b.   Earth
    c.   Air
    d.   Water

3. Is Aries Barren or Fruitful?

4. What planet is in its exaltation in Aries?

5. Is Aries a Cardinal or a Mutable sign?

6. What sign is in its detriment in Aries?

    a.   Venus
    b.   Mars
    c.   Pluto

7. Describe Aries.

8. What signs are Aries attracted to?

9. What is his symbol?

10. In what careers is Aries often found?

11. What herbal remedies are recommended for an Aries?

TAURUS

April 20 – May 20
Ruler: Venus
First of the Earth triplicity
Eastern sign
Fixed sign
Feminine
Semi-fruitful
Short ascension
Planet in exaltation: the Moon
Planet in detriment: Mars
Planet in its fall: Uranus
Archangel: Asmodeus
Angel: Araziel

Taurus, first of the Earth Triplicity and second sign of the zodiac, is ruled by Venus, the planet of love and beauty. A most sensuous creature, she is fond of silks, satins, chocolates, rich foods and most everything that appeals to her five senses. She must discipline herself for she often overindulges. Creative, she is fond of the arts, music and beauty.

She is determined, patient and kind. Like the bull, she endures and possesses a deep well of energy. Practical and trustworthy, she is self-reliant, but stubborn, difficult to budge, and often self-centered. Though she is magnetic, fearless and humorous, she seldom forgets those who have wronged her

Taurus is often susceptible to sore throats, glandular swellings in the neck, mumps, suffocation and strangulation. Fond of her comforts and ease, she may be prone to laziness and obesity. She must avoid fattening foods and exercise moderately.

In love, she is attracted to the earth and water signs of Cancer, Virgo, Scorpio, Capricorn and Pisces. Beware, for though she is loyal and steadfast, she is jealous and possessive. Her subdued nature masks her fiery temper which is not unlike the raging bulls.

Suggested herbs for Taurus:

cedarwood- Effective for bronchial infections. Do not use during pregnancy.

eucalyptus- Effective for colds and the flu. Use in moderation on the skin, but avoid if you have a history of epilepsy. Use with caution if hypertension is present.

ginger- Use for throat infections, congestion, colds and coughs.

marjoram- Use for coughs, colds and bronchitis. Avoid during pregnancy.

myrrh-Use for coughs and sore throat. Do not use during pregnancy.

hyssop- Use as a decongestant for bronchitis, tonsillitis, chest congestion, chest colds and sore throat. Avoid during pregnancy and if you have a history of epilepsy or suffer from hypertension. It is toxic in high concentration.

lavender- use for colds, coughs and flu. Do not use in first trimester of pregnancy.

Questionnaire

1. What is the ruler of Taurus?

2. Does it rule any other sign? If so, what?

3. What planet is in its exaltation in Taurus?

4. What planet is in its detriment in Taurus?

5. What planet is in its fall in Taurus?

6. Describe Taurus.

7. What is the symbol of Taurus?

8. What diseases does Taurus often catch?

9. Name the suggested herbs for Taurus and what they are used for.

GEMINI

May 21-June
Ruler: Mercury
Air Triplicity
Northern sign
Mutable sign
Masculine
Positive
Barren
Short ascension
Double-bodied sign
Planet in exaltation: the Moon's North Node
Planet in detriment: Jupiter
Planet in its fall: the Moon's South Node
Archangel: Ambriel
Angel: Sarayel

Gemini, first of the Air Triplicity, ruled by Mercury, is known for his versatility and love of change. A double-bodied sign, his symbol is the twins. He is ingenious, witty and intellectually curious. Breaking all the rules, he is a nonconformist and a rebel.

Socially, Gemini is a marvelous conversationalist, eloquent and is well liked, particularly by the air and fire signs. He is liberal, highly tolerant, expressive, courageous, generous and sympathetic. Negatively, if his chart indicates a leaning toward dishonesty, he can well be the most cunning and clever of all criminals, often slipping through the authority's fingers.

Gemini's health suffers through mental overstrain, nervousness and restlessness. Because Gemini not only rules the nervous system, but also the lungs, shoulders, collarbones, wrists and hands, he suffers broken bones in these areas due to accidents. He is prone to diseases of the lungs such as asthma, bronchitis, pleurisy and pneumonia.

Attracted to the fire and air signs of Aquarius, Aries, Leo, Libra and Sagittarius, he is a fun-loving companion. Breaking all the rules, he dances to the music that sets his soul free.

Suggested herbs for Gemini:

cypress- for asthma, bronchitis and restlessness. Avoid during pregnancy and if the native suffers from hypertension. Note: Cypress may be used as an insect repellant and to keep pets free of fleas and ticks.

eucalyptus- Use as a respiratory oil, use in moderation on the skin. It relieves asthma, and bronchitis. Do not use if you have a history of epilepsy. Use caution if hypertension is indicated.

hyssop- For asthma and bronchitis. Use in moderation, It is toxic in high concentration. Avoid if you have a history of epilepsy or if you suffer from hypertension.

Questionnaire

1. What planet is the ruler of Gemini?

2. What triplicity does Gemini fit into?

3. What planet or light is in exaltation in Gemini?

4. What planet is in its detriment in Gemini?

5. Describe Gemini.

6. What ailments is Gemini susceptible to?

7. Name the suggested herbs for Gemini and what they are used for.

CANCER

July 21-22
Ruler: the Moon
Water Triplicity
Northern sign
Cardinal sign
Feminine
Negative
Fruitful
Long ascension
Planet in its exaltation: Jupiter
Planet in its detriment: Saturn
Planet in its fall: Mars
Archangel: Muriel
Angel Pakiel

Cancer, ruled by the Moon, is represented by the crab. Known for her domestic and maternal devotion, she is kind, sympathetic, patient and devoted. She is sociable, adaptable and patriotic. As wonderful as these qualities are, no one is perfect. Those born under the sign of Cancer are also moody, changeable, overly sentimental and sensitive.

A Cancer's health often suffers from foods that may not be properly prepared. Caffeine or other stimulants should be avoided. A change of scenery will do wonders for moody Cancer.

In romance, Cancer gravitates toward earth and water signs of Pisces, Taurus, Virgo, Scorpio and Capricorn.

Herbs recommended especially for Cancer:

geranium-since Cancer is subject to many moods, I recommend this herb for emotional balance and depression. Avoid taking in first trimester of pregnancy and do not overuse or the native will become restlessness.

ginger-used for stomach cramps and digestive problems.

lemon- drink fresh lemon juice in water with honey for poor digestion.

marjoram- used in cooking it promotes digestion. Avoid during pregnancy.

Questionnaire

1. What light or planet is the ruler of Cancer?

2.   Of what triplicity does Cancer belong?

3. Is Cancer a Cardinal sign or a Mutable sign?

4. What planet is in its exaltation in Cancer?

5. What planet is in its detriment in Cancer?

6. Describe Cancer.

7. What is the symbol of Cancer?

8. What will help Cancer when he is one of his "moods?"

9. What are the recommended herbs for Cancer?

LEO

July 23 - August 22
The Ruler: the Sun
Fire Triplicity
Northern sign
Fixed sign
Barren
Sign of long ascension
Positive sign
Planet in exaltation: Neptune
Planet in its detriment: Uranus
Planet in its fall: Uranus
Archangel: Verchiel
Angel: Sharatiel

Leo is known to be the king of the zodiac, just as his symbol, the lion, is known to be king of the jungle. Loyal, tolerant, generous and kind, Leo is fearless, energetic, chivalrous and magnetic. He is often found among sports figures, in the entertainment fields, formal gatherings and casinos.

A natural leader, his leadership qualities may manifest as a dictator. Afflicted, Leo can be arrogant, overbearing, domineering and hotheaded.

Ruled by the Sun, he may experience problems with heart disease, heart palpitations, spinal meningitis, sunstrokes and inflammations. He requires harmony and moderation in all things. Excitement must be avoided.

Attracted to the fire and air signs of Aries, Gemini, Libra, Sagittarius and Aquarius, he will entertain and dine his beloved as royalty. Though it is true that opposites attract and often marry, Aquarius, ruled by the planet of Uranus, will not bow down to Leo.

Herbs especially recommended for Leo:

cayenne- for the heart.

digitalis- for the heart.

Questionnaire

1. What light or planet is the ruler of Leo?

2. Is Leo a Fire or a Water sign?

3. Fixed or Mutable?

4. Describe Leo.

5. What careers does Leo gravitate to?

6. What physical problem is Leo prone to?

7. What signs are Leo most attracted to?

VIRGO

August 23- September 22
Ruler: Mercury
Second of the Earth Triplicity
Mutable sign
Northern sign
Barren
Nocturnal
Feminine sign
Negative sign
Sign of long ascension
Planet in exaltation: Mercury
Planet in its detriment: Neptune
Planet in its fall: Venus
Archangel: Hamaliel
Angel: Shelathiel

Virgo, ruled by Mercury, is intelligent, concise, thoughtful, serious and critical. Intuitive, cautious, prudent and industrious, Virgos are meticulous in regard to cleanliness. Fond of travel, literature and conversation, they make excellent nurses, secretaries, editors, fashion designers, and travel agents.

Virgos must pay particular attention to their diet and hygiene in order to avoid bowel disorders such as constipation, peritonitis and malnutrition. A vegetarian diet along with cereal is recommended. Spices should be avoided. Hypochondria is common among this sign.

Because of their critical nature, they may not marry. If they eventually choose a partner, they will prefer an earth or water sign; one who can share their intellectual pursuits. Their choices will fall among Taurus, Cancer, Scorpio, Capricorn and their opposite sign, Pisces.

Herbs recommended for Virgo:

ginger- for stomach cramps, diarrhea or poor digestion.

chamomile- for worries and nervous tension. Avoid during pregnancy.

fennel-for constipation, digestive problems and fluid retention. This herb also assists with kidney functions.

Questionnaire

1. What is Virgo's ruler?

2. What triplicity does Virgo fit into?

3. What planet is in its exaltation in Virgo?

4. What planet is in its detriment in Virgo?

5. Describe Virgo.

6. What careers does Virgo gravitate to?

7. Does Virgo marry often?

8. What are the recommended herbs for Virgo?

LIBRA

September 23-October 22
Ruler: Venus
Second of the Air Triplicity
Cardinal sign
Southern sign
Semi-fruitful
Equinoctial sign
Sign of long ascension
Planet in its exaltation: Saturn
Planet in its detriment: Mars
Planet in its fall: Sun
Archangel: Zuriel
Angel Chedquiel

Libra, ruled by Venus, is a social creature, gravitating to the fine arts, music and beauty. She desires partners and does not like being alone. Vacillating, she weighs the scales, taking time to make her decisions.

She is modest, thoughtful, graceful, adaptable and cheerful. Generous and refined, she is sympathetic and forgives others easily. On the negative side, if her chart is afflicted, she may be indecisive, reckless, hesitant, impressionable, vain, aloof and careless.

A well balanced diet, fresh air, harmonious surroundings and exercise are necessary for her health. Libra rules the kidneys, the ovaries and lumbar vertebrae below the ribs as well as the veins and arteries.

In love, she makes her choices from the air and fire signs of Sagittarius, Aquarius, Aries, Gemini, and Leo. A Libra ascendant will often marry more than once but will have no problem finding another mate among her many friends and social acquaintances.

Recommended herbs:

lemon- for the kidneys. For liver cleansing, drink fresh lemon juice in water with a little honey.

patchouli-for varicose veins, skin allergies, confusion and lethargy. Use only in moderation.

rosemary-a diuretic, astringent. Avoid during pregnancy or with a history of epilepsy.

Questionnaire

1. What is the ruler of Libra?

2. Does its ruler rule any other sign?

3. What triplicity does Libra fall into?

4. Is Libra a fruitful sign?

5. What planet is in its detriment when placed in Libra?

6. Describe Libra.

7. What parts of the body does Libra rule?

8. Name the herbs recommended for Libra.

SCORPIO

October 23- November 21
Ruler: Pluto
Second of the Water Triplicity
Fixed sign
Feminine sign
Negative sign
Long ascension
Fruitful
Planet in exaltation: Uranus
Planet in its detriment: Venus
Planet in its fall: the Moon
Archangel: Barkiel
Angel: Saitziel

Scorpio, second of the Water Triplicity, is one of the strongest signs of the zodiac, running a tie with Leo. Possessing strong willpower, the native is patient, fearless, shrewd and ambitious. Tenacious, she is thoughtful, devoted and eloquent. She will be successful in a career requiring courage, concentration, and perseverance. Scorpio's make excellent surgeons, researchers, detectives, chemists and spies.

On the negative side, if her chart is afflicted by the malefics, Scorpio can be a wicked enemy. Sarcastic, callous, destructive, vindictive and shrewd, she is revengeful. Her health matters often manifest in the reproductive organs and groins.

Her most desirable mates will be found in the earth and water signs of Capricorn, Pisces, Cancer and Virgo. She will inevitably be attracted to her opposite sign, patient fearless, possessive Taurus, the original material girl. Though both signs are passionate and sensual, they are both possessive and jealous. Expect Scorpio to be a high maintenance mate.

Recommended herbs:

mistletoe, horsetail and chamomile to calm Scorpio's strong emotions.

Questionnaire

1. What is the ruler of Scorpio?

2. What type of sign is Scorpio?

3. What planet is in its exaltation in Scorpio?

4. What planet is in its detriment?

5. What planet or light is said to be in its fall in Scorpio?

6. What two signs are said to be the "strongest" in the zodiac?

7. What part of a Scorpio's body do health matters often manifest?

8. What signs are Scorpio most attracted to?

SAGITTARIUS

November 22-December 21
Ruler: Jupiter
Fire Triplicity
Southern sign
Mutable sign
Masculine
Barren sign
Positive sign
Double-bodied sign
Sign of long ascension
Planet in exaltation: the South Node of the Moon
Planet in its detriment: Mercury
Planet in its fall: The North Node of the Moon
Archangel: Adnachiel
Angel: Samequiel

Sagittarius, symbolized as the archer and ruled by Jupiter, is honest, frank, dependable and generous. He is foresighted, jovial, and charitable. Sociable and kindhearted, he is fond of children, pets and sports, particularly auto and horse racing. Ingenious and talented, he will be an excellent politician, social reformer, philosopher or publisher.

He is most at home in the open spaces and participating in out-of- door sports such as horseback riding and hiking. This sign rules the sacrum, the sciatic nerve and the tibia. Since its opposite sign is Gemini, he may suffer from lung and nerve troubles. Rheumatism, gout, dislocation from the hip joint, blood disorders, cuts and wounds are common disorders for Sagittarius.

This sign will choose his friends and mates from the Fire and Air signs of Aquarius, Aries, Libra and his opposite sign, Gemini. On the down side Sagittarius can be a bit pompous, a name dropper. Gemini will not tolerate this, but will puncture Sagittarius's bubble.

Recommended herbs:

cypress, eucalyptus, hyssop, lavender and lemon for rheumatism basil, bergamot, clary-sage for the nerves

rosemary, fennel and juniper for gout.

Questionnaire

1. What planet rules Sagittarius?

2. What triplicity does Sagittarius belong to?

3. What type of sign is Sagittarius? (More than one may apply.)

    a. Mutable
    b. Fixed
    c. Double bodied
    d. Barren

4. What planet is in its detriment in Sagittarius?

5. What careers attract Sagittarius?

6. Describe Sagittarius.

7. What are the herbs recommended for Sagittarius?

CAPRICORN

December 21- January 19
Ruler: Saturn
Earth Triplicity
Cardinal
Feminine
Negative
Short ascension
Planet in exaltation: Mars
Planet in its detriment: the Moon
Planet in its fall: Jupiter
Archangel: Hanael
Angel: Saritiel

Capricorn, third and last of the Earth Ttriplicity, is ruled by Saturn, the grim reaper. She is ambitious, serious, cautious and prudent. This sign needs to stay busy and accomplish. Since her ruler is Saturn, she often has problems with depression and the knees. She requires cheerful companions and a comfortable environment along with out-of-doors exercise.

On the negative side, Capricorns can be selfish, jealous, gloomy, authoritive and suspicious. They may be considered overly conservative, particularly by the fire and air signs. They have a tendency toward bruising easily and are prone to skin diseases, rheumatism, constipation and colds.

For her life's mate, she will carefully choose among the earth and water signs of Pisces, Taurus, Virgo, Scorpio and her opposite sign, Cancer. The opposite signs may balance each other, but there is always a challenge. Capricorn may find Cancer too sensitive for her saturnine nature while Cancer may find the sign too abrasive.

Recommended herbs for Capricorn:

clary sage, bergamot, ylang ylang and jasmine for depression cypress, eucalyptus and hyssop for rheumatism; chamomile and hyssop for bruises.

Questionnaire

1. What is the ruler of Capricorn?

2. What triplicty does Capricorn fit into?

3. What planet is in its exaltation in Capricorn?

4. What planet or light is in its detriment in Capricorn?

5. What planet is in its fall when in Capricorn?

6. Describe Capricorn

7. What signs are Capricorn attracted to?

8. What are the recommended herbs for Capricorn?

AQUARIUS

January 20- February 20
Ruler: Uranus
Air Triplicity
Fixed sign
Masculine
Positive
Short ascension
Southern sign
Planet in exaltation: Uranus
Planet in its detriment: the Sun
Planet in its fall: Neptune
Archangel: Cambiel
Angel: Tzakmiqiel

Freedom loving Aquarius, third of the air signs, ruled by Uranus, is the best friend one could have. He is a humanitarian, a philosopher, progressive, unbiased, intuitive and pleasant. A social being, he is considerate, co-operative, has a fine sense of humor; a beautiful voice and musical ability.

He or she may be a radical or a political extremist. He will derive pleasure from shocking others. He is likely to have sprained and broken bones, suffer from nerve spasms, and impurities of the blood. Though fresh air, water, vegetables and fruit are necessary, fats and greasy foods must be avoided.

Aquarius will choose his mate among the fire and air signs of Aries, Gemini, Libra, and Sagittarius. Though he will be attracted to his opposite sign of Leo and may choose his mate from that particular Sun sign, he will never submit or bow down to Leo, who believes he or she is king or queen of the zodiac. A warning to signs desiring Aquarius for their significant other …freedom-loving Aquarius will not tolerate a jealous mate.

Recommended herbs:

chamomile for calming of the nerves

lavender for nervous tension and rosemary for soothing the nerves.

Questionnaire

1. What is the ruler of Aquarius?

2. What triplicity does Aquarius fit into?

3. What type of sign is Aquarius? Fixed, Mutable or Cardinal?

4. What planet is in its exaltation in Aquarius?

5. In its detriment?

6. In its fall?

7. Describe Aquarius.

8. Name the most common ailments of an Aquarius.

9. What are the recommended herbs for this sign?

PISCES

February 21-March 21
Ruler: Neptune
Water Triplicity
Mutable sign
Feminine
Negative
Short ascension
Eastern sign
Bi-Corporal sign
Planets in exaltation:Venus; Neptune
Planet in its detriment: Mercury
Planet in its fall: Mercury
Angel: Barchiel
Archangel: Amnitziel

Pisces, third of the Water Triplicity, is ruled by nebulous Neptune. Perceptive, refined and inspirational, she is dreamy, easygoing, inspired, hospitable and sensitive. She is honest, kind, possessive, mediumistic and often has psychic abilities.

On the negative side, Pisces is submissive, negative, indecisive, apologetic, and timid and more than likely has an inferiority complex.

She may be found near oceans, fishponds, aquariums, oil fields, churches and at psychic fairs and séances.

She will find her life's love among the water and earth signs of Taurus, Cancer, Virgo, Scorpio and Capricorn. Though she will be attracted to her opposite sign of Virgo, the match will be more challenging than the other earth and water signs.

Recommended herbs:

bergamot, clary sage, jasmine, rose and lavender for mood lifting.

Questionnaire

1. What is the ruler of Pisces?

2. What triplicity does Pisces fit into?

3. Name the planets in exaltation when in Pisces.

4. In its fall?

5. Describe Pisces.

6. Where might I find a Pisces? (Three apply.)

        a.   At a sports arena?
        b.   Near an aquarium?
        c.   An oil field?
        d.   A psychic fair?
        e.   A rodeo?

Chapter 3

THE PLANETS

MARS

Ruler of Aries

Mars, the fourth planet from the Sun, is pure energy. He is action, enterprise, initiative, military, hot, feverish and masculine. In Greek Mythology, Mars signified the God of War. He is strength and desire, accidents, sports and muscle.

Mars is aggressive, headstrong, brave, loud, argumentative, reckless, willful, and daring. He is the warrior, the athlete, the police officer, the firefighter, the wrestler, the dentist, the prizefighter and the middle-aged male. He stands alone, courageous and defiant.

He signifies accidents, danger, fevers, iron, the knife, firearms, the color red, violence and war. Mars also represents dry air, droughts, mild winters, the heating system, fireplaces, stoves and the barbecue cooker. The parts of the body indicated by Mars are the muscles, the body heat and the sexual functions.

Mars in Its Retrograde Position

Mars, ruler of Aries and God of War, is considered the planet of action, aggression and energy. Wherever Mars is in your natal chart will be where you will direct your energy.

For instance, if Mars is positioned in your tenth house natally, you will focus most of your energy on career matters. If it is in your sixth house, you will focus on health matters and the service fields.

In its retrograde position, Mars never actually moves backward, but it appears to do so due to its position in orbit and its relationship to Earth. A benefic planet's influence such as Venus is weakened when it is retrograde; however, the influence of a planet such as Mars is intensified for the eighty days it is retrograde. During the two or three days before and after it is turning, it is said to be in its stationary position. In this position, it is at its strongest.

VENUS

Ruler of Taurus and Libra

Venus, second planet from the Sun, is the ruler of both Taurus and Libra. She bestows a love of beauty, music, poetry and drama as well as refinements to the astrological signs she rules. She is a peacemaker, graceful, sociable, calm and passionate. She rules lower barometers, the skin, the touch, the throat, veins and ovaries. Her colors are the pastel shades of turquoise and crimson. Her day is Friday.

She signifies the sweetheart, the mistress, the kidneys, the ovaries and the veins. She may indicate a vacation, an engagement, a marriage, a honeymoon, a garden or a wedding. Venus also represents the fine arts, flower gardens, family rooms, sitting rooms, furniture, décor, and accessories. Occupations ruled by Venus are dancers, singers, beauticians, artists, jewelers, gardeners, and designers.

If Venus is afflicted in a native's chart, he or she may be lewd, overindulge, display a lack of taste, be lacking in the social refinements as well as have problems with friends, money and love.

While in the sign of Aries, she is in her detriment. Socially, she will not be at ease if her ego is threatened. Though she will have many acquaintances, she will have few real friends. In love, she may chase away those who mean the most to her for she avoids the responsibility of close relationships.

She is in her retrograde position for forty-two days and stationary for approximately two days before and after turning. A benefic planet, she is at her weakest when retrograde. Parts of the body signified by Venus are the veins and the kidneys.

MERCURY

Ruler of Gemini and Virgo

Mercury, first planet from the Sun, represents the intellect, the nervous system, the hands, arms, collarbone and the youth. It also rules the wind, high and low pressures, workshops, utility rooms, entryways, hallways, windows, telephones, modems, remote controls, sewing machines, tools, pet areas and the medicine cabinet. The native ruled by Mercury is quick-witted, exterous, imaginative and analytical. Restless, inquisitive, literate, ingenious and clever, those with Mercury ruling their Sun signs are often found in the fields of publishing, teaching and reporting. They are interviewers, journalists, accountants, writers or editors. As writers, Gemini's tend to write articles or short stories. Most are too restless to write a lengthy manuscript such as a novel.

On the negative side, those ruled by Mercury can also be gossips, glib, forgetful, nervous, worriers, excessively critical, cunning and meddling. Concerned with hygiene and diet, they tend to be hypochondriacs if afflicted, particularly Virgo. Parts of the body signified by Mercury are the speech and hearing organs.

Mercury Retrograde

Mercury moving into its retrograde position is often enough to make one cringe unless the native is aware of the hidden benefits.

During the time Mercury is in its apparent retrograde motion, there will be mechanical problems and a breakdown of communications. Computers, telephones and faxes are often affected as well as small appliances and motor vehicles. Traveling will be difficult with delays and accidents. Give yourself more time while in transit, be patient and realize that many people are distracted and in a hurry.

The phrase, "Mercury retrograde", leads one to believe that the planet is actually traveling backward motion. All planets but the Sun and Moon are said to go into retrograde motion, but no planet actually does. They appear to because of their position in orbit and their relationship to Earth. The influence of the planet doesn't change, but our reactions are different. The astrological house the planet is transiting through in your chart is the area of your life that will be affected.

In an astrologer's ephemeris, the planets positions are recorded by sign and degree. When it appears to be in its retrograde motion, it is indicated by the symbol R/. When it appears to be direct, it is indicated by the symbol D/. When neither in R/ or D/ motion, it is said to be stationary. When in its stationary position, it is at its strongest.

Approximately three times a year, Mercury is in its retrograde position for twenty-four days. It is important to allow two days before and after its turning for prediction purposes. Avoid signing contracts while Mercury is retrograde; otherwise, expect revisions when the planet moves direct.

While Mercury is in its retrograde position, slow down, finish projects and re-evaluate the specific area of your life Mercury retrograde is affecting. Postpone major decisions or new beginnings until after Mercury has turned direct.

Remember to allow two days before and after a planet turns. Events will not completely return to normal until the planet catches up to the degree it went retrograde at.

THE MOON

Ruler of Cancer

The Moon, the smaller luminary of the Earth, makes one revolution through the astrological chart every twenty-seven days, seven hours and forty-three minutes. During that time, it triggers events, moods, health conditions and psychological states of mind.

It represents the emotions, the past, memories, relationships and all that is feminine as well as the baby, the breasts, the bathroom, conception, evening, family, groceries, home, kitchen, lake, liquids, melons, milk, the mother, nutrition, the public, the saloon, restaurant, stomach, tides, baker, caterer, cook, grocer, the nurse, the midwife, milkman, the nation, and the queen. The Moon also represents the dining room, bowls, cups, the bathtub, vegetable gardens, the bedroom and your personal bed.

Natives ruled by the Moon, either born under the Sun sign of Cancer or born with a Cancer ascendant are often psychic and mediumistic.

Well aspected, there is often gain through public work, property and real estate.

Biologically, the Moon represents fertility, body fluids, and the lymph or the cerebellum. It never goes into a retrograde position or remains stationery.

THE SUN
Ruler of Leo

The Sun, Earth's larger luminary and ruler of Leo, transits all of the signs of the zodiac in one year and enters each sign on approximately the twenty-first of the month. Aspected well and unafflicted from other planets, the Sun bestows ambition, pride and honor to its natives. Afflicted, the native may be arrogant, with a forceful and domineering personality.

The Sun is dignified, haughty, animated, cooperative, and joyful. Loyal, majestic, radiant, virile, and often famous, natives ruled by the Sun may be actors, supervisors, athletic directors, sports stars or coaches.

The Sun signifies the atmosphere, ego drive, personal identity, the father, the husband, the king, the boss, daylight, faith, fire, gold, health, heart, the lion, the mansion, the front door, lighting, light fixtures, large paintings or pictures, children's rooms and musical instruments, noon, orange, the peacock, the president, the prince, the starfish, Sunday, and the throne. Biologically, the Sun represents the heart. Just as the Moon, the Sun does not go into a stationary or retrograde position.

PLUTO
Ruler of Scorpio

Pluto, the last planet from the Sun, is a planet of extremes. It rules the masses and is violent, yet charismatic, destructive, yet spiritually evolved. Pluto may rule a native who is a surgeon or one who is ruthless. He rules the underworld, the conscience and subconscious activities.

He is callous, corrupt, defiant, insatiable, lawless, obscene, outrageous, passionate, sexual, unscrupulous and vindictive. He represents the psychoanalyst, the abyss, the bomb, the crematory, dice, holocaust, lust, magic, the monster, the racketeer, a siren, the vampire, vermin, victim, the virus, plumbing, toilets, hot water heaters, drains, basements, chimneys and garbage disposals.

Pluto represents transformation and regeneration. Natives ruled by Pluto may have an uncanny, near magical influence over the masses. They may be public speakers, politicians, detectives, spies, or actors.

When in its retrograde position, it affects our subconscious more deeply than usual. It is also indigitive of psychic powers we have retained from other lifetimes that may be used positively in this life, especially through service to others.

JUPITER

Ruler of Sagittarius

Jupiter's symbol is the archer. He represents wealth, self-confidence and respectability. He loves out-of-door sports, horses, horse races and auto races. He is benevolent, expanding, optimistic, sociable, jovial, compassionate, spiritual, honest, just and noble. He is masculine, moderate, philosophical, humorous, extravagant, indulgent, generous, magnificent, peaceful, professional and successful. If Jupiter is conjunct or favorably aspecting your Sun or ascending sign, you may gain weight.

Jupiter signifies abscesses, the blood, recklessness, hazards, waste, judgments, juries, legacies, ransom, surplus, Thursday, thunder, warts, whales, long voyages, large rooms, exercise rooms or gyms, the backyard and mobile homes. The planet is retrograde 120 days and is stationary approximately five days before and after it turns.

Those born under the ruler of Sagittarius are often ambassadors, bankers, brokers, diplomats, gamblers, judges, lawyers, ministers, physicians and publishers. Jupiter represents the liver and gallbladder. In regard to weather forecasts, Jupiter is considered to be fair weather, bringing temperate conditions.

SATURN

Ruler of Capricorn

Saturn, ruler of Capricorn, is the oppressor. He will restrict, limit and destroy. He is frigid, intense, severe and demands introspection and prudence. An overly proud native will suffer a long fall and be brought to his very knees by negative Saturn transits. In time, once Saturn's wrath eases, his victim will realize that his oppressor has been his redeemer.

Natives born under the rule of Saturn are economical, serious, practical and conservative. They are sensitive, but will hide their emotions under a cloak of reserve. When Saturn is afflicted in their chart, they will have delays, restrictions, disappointments, and heartbreaks leading the native to a life filled with misery and often poor health. Saturn's transits are especially difficult for adults of ages twenty-nine to thirty, fifty-nine to sixty and eighty-seven to eighty-eight.

Salvation for his victims will be found in bright airy new places, with light-hearted companions and metaphysical treatments.

Saturn rules the knees, teeth, bones, rheumatism, the foundation of buildings, the basement slab, walls, dividers, main beams, supports, the landlord and the refrigerator. His natives are found working in cemeteries, prisons, seminaries and coal mines. He is a mason, a leather worker, a farmer or a cement worker. In regard to weather, Saturn represents cold, damp conditions. Storms or low-pressure systems occurring under a Saturn influence may last longer and span a wider area.

Retrograde for one hundred and forty days, Saturn is stationary for approximately five days before and after turning. When the planet is in its retrograde position, its malice is increased. Parts of the body Saturn represents are the bone structure and the knees.

URANUS

Ruler of Aquarius

Uranus, ruler of Aquarius, is considered the most unusual planet. Rotating from north to south, rather than east to west as other planets do, he rolls around the Sun while his satellites revolve around him in retrograde motion .

He is unconventional, ingenious, enthusiastic, musical, intuitive, innovative and freedom loving. He possesses metaphysical abilities and is often clairvoyant.

He may be misunderstood and considered eccentric, extreme, erratic or radical, but he is the humanitarian of the zodiac.

Often natives ruled by Uranus are electricians, inventors, astrologers, broadcasters, X-ray technicians, auto mechanics and computer techs.

Uranus signifies radical or sudden change: cold, dry air; high barometers; high winds; wiring, all electrical devices, electronic appliances to include radios, computers, microwaves; group spaces; lightning; batteries; disasters; tornados; vapors; radioactive materials; magnets; firecrackers; divorce; crises; cyclones; earthquakes; electronics; microscopes; outlaws; revolts; uranium, and whirlwinds.

When in its retrograde position, there is a difficulty expressing originality. A renewal of ideas from past lives may surface. Karmic family and social problems re-occur, perhaps in order to solve and better serve the family or community. The parts of the body Uranus represents are the pituitary gland, connections with the nervous system, membranes of the brain, and spinal marrow.

NEPTUNE

Ruler of Pisces

Neptune, God of the Sea, and ruler of Pisces is mystical, psychic, spiritual, romantic, sensitive and reserved. Under Neptune's influence, one may absorb the influence or vibrations of those around him. Negatively, the native ruled by Neptune may become psychically disturbed.

Harmoniously aspected, those ruled by Neptune receive premonitions and are prompted to be in the right place at the right time. They are clairvoyant and psychic, and often multi-talented. Neptune is beguiling, dreamy, emotional, exotic, glamorous, imaginative, mysterious, naïve, poetic, receptive, tranquil and visionary.

Natives of Neptune are often divers, mediums, oil field workers, poets, psychics, musicians, sorcerers, liquor store owners and magicians. Neptune signifies alcohol, lower barometers, torrential downpours, floods. drugs, closets, floors, carpets, libraries, the shower, swimming pool, roof, drainage, leaks, an astral voyage, beach, body of water, fog, fantasy, gasoline, kerosene, hallucination, intrigue, oil, opiate, poisons, prophecy, oracle, scandal, seclusion, trance, the unconscious, the pineal gland, solar plexus and the aura. Ethereal Neptune bestows mystical dreams and fantasies upon his natives; however, during a Neptune retrograde transit, religious shams are often exposed.

Questionnaire

1. What sign does Mars rule?

2. Describe Mars

3. What careers does one with Mars in Aries gravitate to?

4. What parts of the body does Mars rule?

5. What is a retrograde position?

6. What sign or signs does Venus rule?

7. Describe Venus and what she signifies.

8. What careers attracts one with a prominent Venus?

9. Does Venus move into a retrograde position?

10. If so, does the planet actually move backwards?

11. If Venus does move into a retrograde position, for how long?

12. What parts of the body does Venus rule?

Chapter 4

THE PLANETS IN THE SIGNS

PLANETS IN ARIES

The Sun in Aries
"I Am"

The Sun in Aries is enthusiastic, impulsive and courageous. He dares to go where angels fear to tread, is passionate, headstrong and enterprising. He is a natural born leader and does not like to be told what to do. He is quick tempered, rash and willful. He resents imposition, but doesn't hold a grudge long. He is self-willed, likely to go to extremes, and is not easily discouraged. He is at his best when he is in control.

The Moon in Aries

The Moon in Aries is impulsive, hasty, rash, acts without thinking first and does not like to be told what to do. He or she has a strong personality, is forceful, courageous, restless, quick-tempered and aggressive. Energetic and inventive, the native is at his best in independent ventures or at the head of things, yet the native who has his Moon in Aries does not always finish what he or she sets out to do.

If the Moon is afflicted, the native must be careful around water. Trouble may arise through women and changes of occupation. This position indicates headaches.

Mercury in Aries

Mercury in Aries is quick-witted, excellent in debates yet often antagonistic and contentious. Demonstrative, he is likely to exaggerate.

He is clever, unique, inventive and interesting. Fond of reading, writing and literature, he enters new projects quickly. He or she is restless, nervous and demonstrates a lack of mental continuity as his mind skips from one subject to another.

Venus in Aries

Venus is in her detriment in Aries. He or she falls in love at first sight, is demonstrative, affectionate, warmhearted and attracted to friends of the opposite sex. Popular, she has many friends. She is sympathetic and generous, giving freely to those less fortunate. He or she hastily involves himself or herself in love adventures, is a romantic dreamer and often has an early marriage. She enjoys travel, painting, sculpture, singing, poetry and the theatre. On the negative side, there is often marital disharmony.

Mars in Aries

Mars, at home in Aries, is forceful, self-assured, combative, enthusiastic, and independent. Possessing a pioneering spirit, he is ambitious, impatient, impulsive and argumentative. He is an adventurer, a sportsman, a natural mechanic and an explorer. If afflicted, he will have a ferocious temper, a scar on the face and problems with his eyes.

Saturn in Aries

Saturn in Aries is in its fall, but the native has good reasoning power, is industrious, perseverant, and contemplative. He is diligent, ambitious and desires to make his own way. He can be self-willed, defiant, selfish and contentious. A jealous partner, he or she often has difficulties in marriage. Most of his or her problems occur in the first half of his life.

Jupiter in Aries

Jupiter in Aries is honest, noble and generous. He is progressive, ambitious, philosophical and responsible. He enjoys science, literature, travel, horses and out-of- door exercises and sports. He may benefit through influential friends, law, religious associates, children, speculation and insurance. His home is often beautifully furnished and arranged.

Uranus in Aries

Uranus, a slow moving outer planet, was transiting Aries during the years of 1844 to 1859 and again in 1927 to1935. A love of independence, freedom, and reform is present in this position. Mentally active, the natives with Uranus in Aries are original and inventive, fond of machinery and electrical devices. A love of travel is apparent as well as many changes in residence. The native may be tactless, stubborn, and violent, lacking self-control. Many estrangements are indicated during his or her lifetime.

Neptune in Aries

Neptune, a slow moving outer planet, was positioned in Aries during the years of 1861 to 1875. Natives born with Neptune in Aries are interested in secret societies, social welfare and psychic research. This position intensifies the emotions and senses. The native with Neptune in Aries is sympathetic and benevolent. Original ideas in regard to religious matters may rise to the forefront as well as a desire to reform human conditions and existing institutions. On the negative side, there is a desire for the excessive use of stimulants and gratification of sensual desires.

Pluto in Aries

Pluto, a slow moving outer planet, spends twelve to thirty years in one sign. From approximately 1822 to1851, it was in Aries. During the time Pluto is transiting the sign of Aries, politicians, public speakers and propagandists are likely to be born. These natives more than likely, will be revolutionary, inventive and eccentric. A native born with Pluto in Aries will possess qualities for leadership and the charisma needed to influence the masses in an effort to present and carry forth their revolutionary ideas.

PLANETS IN TAURUS

Sun in Taurus
"I Have"

The Sun is positioned in Taurus from approximately April 21 to May 21. Taurians are patient, cautious, determined, secretive, reserved, and self-reliant. They are known to be gentle creatures, but furious when their anger is aroused.

They are artistic, musical, love nature and literature. Psychic, many are healers and mediums.

Moon in Taurus

Moon in Taurus is warmhearted, tenacious and courteous with an easygoing disposition that inclines toward friendship, love and marriage. Their sympathies are easily aroused. Moon in Taurus has businesses or homes near the water and are inclined to acquire possessions, homes and land even though their material circumstances are changeable.

Mercury in Taurus

Mercury in Taurus is fond of his pleasures, comforts, music and the arts. He has a logical mind, good judgment and is pleasant. Deliberating and patient, once he has made up his mind, he is determined, has set opinions and can be obstinate. If he speaks for too long at a time, his voice may become hoarse.

Venus in Taurus

Venus in Taurus is affectionate and has deep feelings. She is conservative, correct in social situations and faithful. She has a love of wealth, luxuries and precious gem stones. This position indicates gains through legacies and marriage though marriage may come later in life.

Mars in Taurus

Mars in Taurus is ambitious, foresighted, determined and persistent. He is tactful, diplomatic and self-confident. His temper, when aroused, is violent. If the chart is afflicted, he will have legal and financial difficulties, strong opponents or enemies, loss of legacies and scandals.

Mars in Taurus, if afflicted natally, will be extraordinarily forceful with a violent temper. He will inevitably have difficulties through marriage, partnerships and the opposite sex.

Saturn in Taurus

Saturn in Taurus is stubborn, resentful, quiet, prudent, diplomatic and reserved in regard to his own financial affairs. He is quick-tempered, economical, thrifty, inhibited and stubborn. While he is fond of botany and breeding livestock, he has a drive to acquire property. He may have unfortunate domestic experiences and suffer loss through relatives when Saturn is afflicted.

Jupiter in Taurus

Jupiter in Taurus is generous, just, affectionate, peaceful and reserved. This position often indicates a trusteeship as well as an interest in financial matters and philosophy. The native may gain through legacies, speculation, marriage and partnerships as well as all things ruled by Taurus. If afflicted, he will suffer losses of these things.

Uranus in Taurus

Uranus was transiting Taurus approximately during the years of 1850 to1859 and again in 1934 to1942. Natives born with Uranus in Taurus are determined, resourceful, ingenious, intuitive and interested in the occult. Marriage often brings jealousy on the side of the partner. Financial affairs are erratic through he or she may gain through inventions, and originality. He enjoys speculation and is particularly resourceful in earning money, doing so in unusual ways and in all things ruled by Uranus.

Neptune in Taurus

Neptune was in the sign of Taurus approximately from 1874 to 1889. While Neptune was transiting Taurus, there was a gain in speculation and in secret organizations. An individual with Neptune in Taurus is drawn to the occult, the mystical and to antique jewelry. He is patient and enthusiastic in his beliefs. Though he enjoys seclusion and may turn away from conventional trends, he will be a good companion or mate.

Pluto in Taurus

Pluto was in its detriment in Taurus in 1851 through approximately 1882. The planet moves slowly and will not return to Taurus until well after 2050. While Pluto was transiting Taurus, there were new inventions, colonial expansion and development in natural resources. Standards of living improved.

PLANETS IN GEMINI

The Sun in Gemini
"I Think"

Vivacious, versatile, ever-changing Gemini is adaptable, restless and yearns to travel and explore. His symbol, the twins, represents a person able to see both sides of an issue. His mind is active, quick and may jump rapidly from subject to subject. Gemini is a mental air sign, producing many writers and editors. Studious, imaginative and idealistic, he has an active mind and responds well in emergencies. This sign engages in more than one occupation at a time.

The Moon in Gemini

Moon in Gemini's moods are like quicksilver-changing rapidly. She has many female friends, interests, hopes and wishes. Responsive to new ideas, she often speaks fluently on local or national affairs though she prefers to keep her own private. On the go and physically active, she is usually found in professional occupations.

Mercury in Gemini

Ingenious, quick and clever, Mercury in Gemini is inventive and resourceful. Excellent in business, he is adaptable and has an inventive mind. Expect Mercury in Gemini to be on the go. He loves traveling, change and the newness or novelty of different places and cultures. He enjoys literature, science and the occult. On the negative side, he needs to practice tidiness, perseverance and patience. He must not overwork or a nervous breakdown is quite possible.

Venus in Gemini

Charming, courteous, witty, friendly and cooperative, Venus in Gemini's emotions are ruled by the mind. Her love relationships may be superficial. She is able to see people as they actually are. This quality is one that makes an excellent writer or speaker. Talented and amusing, she is a delightful entertainer and may have more than one source of income or occupation. An intellectual, she is inventive, good- humored and social. A native with Venus placed in Gemini may have dual love affairs and more than one mate in his or her lifetime.

Mars in Gemini

Mars in Gemini has a sharp mind, is witty, but tends to be argumentative and sarcastic. Restless, he tends to scatter his energies. Fond of chemistry, lectures, science, travel and law, he has an inventive mind. He is practical and able to make quick decisions. If afflicted, he may have problems with neighbors, writings, education, traveling. He may be separated from his siblings, have problems with his lungs, hands, arms, shoulders or collar bone. Mars in Gemini, like Venus in Gemini, tends to have more than one mate and may marry a relative.

Saturn in Gemini

Saturn in Gemini is shy and awkward in his social life. He has a logical mind, is capable of deep study and may produce major literary and intellectual achievements. He is resourceful, adaptable, ingenious and may also succeed as a teacher or lecturer particular in the scientific or mathematic fields. If afflicted, problems may arise with relatives, legal affairs or neighbors. Because this native tends to be a pessimist, he needs to lean to have faith in the future.

Jupiter in Gemini

Jupiter in Gemini is a carefree spirit, loves change, and desires many social contacts. Courteous and honest, Jupiter in Gemini is a trustworthy soul, fond of travel, intellectual pursuits and delving into the occult. More than likely, he will be successful in the fields of writing, publishing, business or mathematics. Jupiter placed in this sign may have more than one mate during his lifetime. If Jupiter in Gemini is afflicted, he may choose an unpopular or unprofitable occupation. Problems may arise from publishing.

Uranus in Gemini

During the years of 1858 to 1866 and 1941 to 1949, Uranus was transiting the sign of Gemini bestowing traits of originality, versatility and intuition upon its natives. A native with Uranus in Gemini enjoys the study of electricity, aerodynamics, astrology, metaphysics and science. He enjoys traveling to unusual places and is often telepathic or clairvoyant. If afflicted, he may have an unusual or erratic education, may be separated from his siblings or have problems with his neighbors.

Neptune in Gemini

Neptune was transiting the sign of Gemini during the years of 1887 to 1902. Natives born during these years were imaginative and prophetic. They possessed an interest in science, mathematics, poetry, philosophy, drama and the occult. They were skilled conversationalists and adept at producing fine-handiwork.

Pluto in Gemini

Pluto was transiting the sign of Gemini during the years of 1881 to 1912. During those years, major inventions in communication and transportation occurred. Scientists, organizers and adventurers met with success. We experienced the abolition of censorship and the development of colloquial patterns of speech. When Pluto was afflicted, ruthless behavior was displayed in regard to society.

PLANETS IN CANCER

The Sun in Cancer
"I Feel"

The Sun is positioned in the sign of Cancer from approximately June 21 until July 21. Cancer's symbol is the crab. The native is moody and often lectures when it isn't necessary. He or she is reserved, contemplative, enjoys being at home. Do not criticize his friends or family. He will not allow this from anyone but himself.

Moon in Cancer

Moon in Cancer is affectionate, friendly, family oriented, domestic and economical. Sensitive, she is reserved and impressionable. Moody and easily hurt, she will always remember a cruel word or action. Her lesson is to forgive and forget. Although Moon in Cancer seeks peace and quiet, she often finds herself the focus of attention. Afflicted, she will suffer indigestion and stomach problems.

Mercury in Cancer

Mercury in Cancer is perceptive, diplomatic, discreet, sensitive, psychic, mediumistic and sympathetic. Intuitive, the native may become easily depressed over their own and others problems. Becoming emotionally involved, they are able to arouse others sympathies. Because of this quality, they may become excellent public speakers influencing others. They have a sense of harmony; are often talented and interested in art, genealogy, music, and psychic investigation.

Venus in Cancer

Venus in Cancer is domestic, sympathetic, kind-hearted, and loving with a strong tie to her mother. Imaginative and receptive, he or she may have secret love affairs and attractions to those who are of a considerable age difference, perhaps to one who is involved in metaphysics or one with the occult. The native with Venus in Cancer is changeable, artistic, enjoys music and entertaining lavishly in her home. She must not allow others to take advantage of her. When she is upset or feels neglected and unloved, she may experience stomach problems.

Mars in Cancer

Mars in Cancer is in its fall. Ambitious, sympathetic, moody, defensive, and overemotional, the native displays a lack of self control. Bold, fearless and independent, Mars in Cancer holds emotional hurts for a long time. He is fond of luxury, and items connected to the home. If this position is well aspected, the native may gain through voyages and business enterprises connected with the public. If afflicted, the native's home and domestic life may become a battleground or it may be damaged or destroyed through natural disasters. The mother may have an early death. Troubles with the public, women and inheritances may occur. Many changes in residences are indicated. Physically, the native will have problems with indigestion and the stomach.

Saturn in Cancer

Saturn in Cancer is reserved, protective and has strong psychic abilities. Often insecure, the native worries about his family and whether he is a good parent. Becoming emotionally depressed easily, he fears being hurt by others. Though kind, he may lack empathy. If afflicted, family ties and domesticity may cause the native problems and irritations. Hypersensitive, he may become discontented easily. When Saturn is transiting the sign of Cancer, use extra caution if you wish to invest in the stock market.

Jupiter in Cancer

Jupiter in Cancer is receptive, ambitious, enterprising, sympathetic and charitable. Well liked among his social circle, he draws the attention of the public. Imaginative and intuitive, he is fond of the fine arts, the home and mother. He enjoys long voyages overseas and may travel for his health or for educational purposes. He may gain through the public, domestic affairs or inheritance. On the negative side, he is impressionable and may easily be led astray.

Uranus in Cancer

Uranus transited the sign of Cancer from approximately 1865 to 1872 and 1948 to 1956. Natives born with Uranus in Cancer are patriotic and display an interest in legislative activities. They possess mediumistic qualities, a strong imagination and for the most part, are sensitive, restless, impatient and radical. They may be insecure and must guard against the tendency to become easily swayed by their emotions. Their home and domestic life may be erratic. Stomach problems are probable as well as unexpected losses through home, land and property.

Neptune in Cancer

Neptune was transiting the sign of Cancer from 1901 to 1915. Natives born with Neptune transiting the sign of Cancer are intuitive, psychic and mediumistic. Attached to their family and particularly their mother, they are affectionate, capable of deep feelings, but also hypersensitive. Preferring to see the world through rose colored glasses, they have an inclination to overindulge in drugs or alcohol. These natives are compassionate and demonstrate unselfishness in serving others.

Pluto in Cancer

Pluto was in Cancer from approximately 1912 to 1939. World War 1 was taking place and another, World War 11, was beginning. Homes were transformed. Hearts were broken as loved ones were killed, separated and lost. Divorce was on the up-swing and women became emancipated. Natives born during these years are intuitive, physic, patriotic, and feel a responsibility to the world. They are contemplative and have a desire to strike out and research the unknown.

PLANETS IN LEO

Sun in Leo
"I Will"

The Sun moves into the sign of Leo on July 21 and remains there until August 21. Second of the fire signs, Leo is a masculine and positive sign. Natives of Leo are creative, entertaining, vital, confident and generous. On the negative side, they can be arrogant, conceited, aggressive and bossy. At their best, they bring sunshine and laughter into others lives. You will often find them in the fields of entertainment, leadership and sports.

Moon in Leo

The Moon positioned in Leo is intuitive, easily hurt, creative, generous, passionate, and social. She is society's queen as well as the mistress of love. She enjoys luxury and being amused. At her worst, she is snobbish and vain. She desires attention and needs to realize that money and the luxuries it can afford her are not the most important things in life.

Mercury in Leo

Creative, enthusiastic and speculative, Mercury in Leo is an entertaining and articulate speaker. Possessing leadership qualities and desiring attention, he may become over impressed with himself and his ideas. He will expect adoration for everything he does, thinks or says. He is prudent; far-sighted and possesses organizing ability.

Venus in Leo

Venus in Leo is warmhearted, sensitive and desires love and attention. They often feel they are never loved enough. You cannot give Venus in Leo enough attention. They enjoy luxuries, fine clothing, entertainment, pleasures and amusements.

Mars in Leo

Mars in Leo is self-confident, self-assured, willing to take a chance, enterprising, enthusiastic and ambitious. He may also be egotistical, jealous, and bossy. Afflicted, he may have heart problems.

Saturn in Leo

Saturn in Leo is strong willed, efficient, conservative, loyal, introverted and diplomatic. He or she has difficulties with love and in expressing himself or herself. He appears to be cold and often lives a life of isolation.

Jupiter in Leo

Jupiter in Leo is optimistic, generous, and desires admiration. He is speculative, a farsighted leader and executive. He enjoys luxury and wealth. Popular, especially among high society, he may be vain and egotistical.

Uranus in Leo

Uranus in Leo is an adventurer and a gambler. He is bold, enterprising and desires freedom. His tastes in pleasures and entertainment are eclectic and unusual as are his love affairs. He enjoys being different and wears more flamboyant colors and clothing than most. He is often a leader, a revolutionary and cannot abide restriction.

Neptune in Leo

Neptune in Leo is creative and warmhearted. Romantic and susceptible to flattery, they enjoy the social life, traveling, drinking and every kind of pleasure imaginable. They are the escapists of the zodiac and delight in all types of entertainments, particularly the theatre, movies, television and musical plays. Living in their make-believe world of pleasures, they are seductive and wasteful creatures at their worst. At their best, they can curb the negative aspects, leading and inspiring others, just as Shirley Temple Black, Judy Garland and Margot Fonteyn did. Billy Graham and Martin Luther King, both admirable men, were born with Neptune in Leo.

Pluto in Leo

Pluto in was in the sign of Leo from 1938 to 1957. Briefly, it went into retrograde motion into Cancer during February of 1939 until mid-June of that year. While it was positioned in the sign of Leo, the United Nations was formed, governments and dictators rose and fell, and atomic energy was discovered. The entertainment industry went through a transformation as television was developed. Natives born with Pluto in Leo are confident and creative, capable of extraordinary accomplishments, but may have a tendency to be ruthless.

PLANETS IN VIRGO

Sun in Virgo
"I Analyze"

From approximately August 23 until September 23, the Sun is in the second Earth sign of Virgo. Ruled by Mercury, Sun in Virgo is shy, reserved, considerate, reliable, analytical and diligent. On the negative side, they are perfectionists, worriers, and find fault with most everything. Because worry causes tension which affects their health, they may be afflicted with intestinal problems and ulcers. If they do not develop a positive outlook, they may become hypochondriacs. Particularly interested in health, they are often found at health fairs and health food stores. Virgos generally enter the service field and become excellent nurses, secretaries, accountants, teachers and craftsman. Attracted to the earth and water signs of Taurus, Cancer, Scorpio and Capricorn, they have difficulty in expressing themselves when they are in love. Though they will inevitably be attracted to their opposite sign of Pisces, the dual sign of the fish may find Virgo distant, his emotions too cool.

Moon in Virgo

Moon in Virgo is practical, methodical, considerate, diligent and orderly. They may be grocers, managers or housekeepers. Analytical, they have problems understanding people and become critical of them. In romance, this native's head rules his heart.

Mercury in Virgo

Diligent, analytical and patient, he enjoys learning. Mercury in Virgo, though critical, usually makes a good team-worker. Health-wise, he may have digestive problems due to his sedentary lifestyle.

Venus in Virgo

An excellent teacher and homemaker, a person who has Venus placed in Virgo is likely to want everything neat and clean. He or she is kind and sympathetic but doesn't want to become involved. Practical considerations overrule matters of the heart. Since they have problems expressing their affection, they continually encounter problems in their love life.

Mars in Virgo

Mars in Virgo is kind and even tempered. A worrier, he tends to be irritable, nervous and critical. A methodical worker, he is good with detail work and possesses a love of tidiness. A native whose Mars is placed in Virgo does not like assuming more than his share of responsibility. Worry may cause him stomach problems and a breaking out of the skin.

Saturn in Virgo

Saturn remains in a zodiac sign for two years. In general, a native whose Saturn is placed in Virgo is meticulous, correct, and serious. He is discreet and will assume his share of responsibility. On the negative side, if Saturn is afflicted, the native may be a nag and be misunderstood.

Jupiter in Virgo

A person whose Jupiter is placed in the sign of Virgo is practical, curious and intellectual. Possessing organizational abilities and high moral values, he would make an excellent teacher. The problem with this position is that the native may become cynical or critical. If he becomes too involved with the immediate, he may forget the need to nourish his soul.

Uranus in Virgo

Uranus is a generational aspect, taking eighty-four years to revolve around our Sun. While it is transiting Virgo, its natives are often born with a sharp mind and a desire for perfection. Many are interested in natural healing and herbal remedies. They are cautious and discriminating, yet choose unusual professions.

Neptune in Virgo

Gentle and patient, natives with Neptune placed in Virgo, are reserved, interested in all things psychic, and may possess an ability to communicate with those spirits who have passed on before us.

Conscientious of hygiene and diet, he may be a vegetarian and interested herbal remedies.

Pluto in Virgo

The native whose Pluto is placed in the zodiac sign of Virgo often has a curious mind, is analytical, critical of social conditions and interested in new methods of healing. They have a drive for perfection. During 1957 to 1972, when Pluto was transiting Virgo, computers were invented. The Common Market was founded and free trade went into effect.

PLANETS IN LIBRA

Sun in Libra
"I Balance"

A native whose Sun is placed in the sign of Libra is sociable, harmonious and creative. He is adaptable, enjoys the fine arts and has fine manners and social skills. Associations are important to one whose Sun is in Libra. On the negative side, he lacks consistency and has a difficult time making decisions.

Moon in Libra

A native whose Moon is placed in Libra desires love and affection. Sociable creatures, they express their feelings warmly. Desiring to be liked by everyone, they seek peace. Though they are the masters of tact and diplomacy, they must learn to hold true to their principles.

Mercury in Libra

Artistic, Mercury in Libra may be an excellent speaker, aware of both the pros and cons of a subject he wishes to discuss. He is adaptable with a sense of beauty and balance. Tactful and diplomatic, he works well with partners.

Venus in Libra

One with Venus placed in the sign of Libra is refined, sociable, and often possesses music and artistic abilities. A romantic at heart, she is easily hurt. If she is not married, she may have a tendency to scatter her affections. Married, she may attempt to conform her partner.

Mars in Libra

Mars placed in the air sign of Libra is said to be in his detriment. Though one who has Mars placed in Libra is perceptive and easygoing, he can be argumentative. He is neither diplomatic, nor patient, but he is enthusiastic.

Saturn in Libra

One whose Saturn is placed in Libra may display a strong sense of duty and reliability, especially toward partnerships.

Jupiter in Libra

The native whose Jupiter is placed in the sign of Libra is sincere, mild, conscientious, fond of travel, music and the fine arts. He is often held in high esteem and receives many honors during his life. This is an excellent position for an attorney or a judge.

Uranus in Libra

Artistically talented and creative, one with Uranus in Libra desires to carry out reforms in the sole interest of the public. He may have unusual ideas about marriage and partnerships. Negatively aspected, he will not be as adaptable as most Libras.

Neptune in Libra

Those born with Neptune in Libra are artistic with high ideals. Desiring harmony, peace and justice, they enjoy being an active part of the community. Unfortunately, many with this placement are easily deceived. When set upon by external pressures, they may have difficulties maintaining mental stability and need to gain a sense of identity.

Pluto in Libra

Pluto transited the sign of Libra from 1972 to1984. During those years, we saw changes in laws such as birth control, death and marriage. New concepts in art were introduced during these years which had a psychic emphasis designed to uplift one's spirit. Those born with Pluto transiting Libra are adaptable and cooperative though they may have a tendency to be insincere and evasive.

PLANETS IN SCORPIO

"Involvement"
Sun in Scorpio

With the Sun placed in the sign of Scorpio, natives are passionate, fearless yet oftentimes overestimate themselves. Possessing a tremendous amount of will-power, they may struggle with their own existence. Through effort and tenacity, they will succeed and maintain their position in life.

Moon in Scorpio

One born with the Moon transiting the sign of Scorpio may be easily hurt, prone to emotional extremes. Vindictive, they must learn forgiveness. Energetic, independent, aggressive and determined, they would benefit from channeling their emotions into a creative outlet.

Mercury in Scorpio

The native born with Mercury in Scorpio possesses positive qualities such as perseverance and endurance when pursuing difficult problems. On the other hand, he or she may be sarcastic, skeptical and crafty. When afflicted, Mercury in Scorpio may be argumentative and prone to fighting.

Venus in Scorpio

Creative and passionate, one who has Venus transiting the sign of Scorpio in their natal chart has a tendency to be unreasonably jealous and uninhibited. This is said to be a karmic placement and requires the native to learn the lesson of self-control. There may be a legacy due to Venus in Scorpio, but he or she may have problems obtaining it.

Mars in Scorpio

Mars in Scorpio may be forceful and determined, disregarding the feelings of others. Investigative and intelligent, he is prone to be overbearing and vindictive. This placement may be beneficial for surgeons, chemists and those involved in investigative work.

Jupiter in Scorpio

Jupiter placed in the sign of Scorpio in one's chart lends an optimistic attitude toward the native's life. He may be efficient, hardworking, with a flair for finance. Secretive, he possesses a great deal of magnetism and healing ability. With this placement, it is important that the native strive to assist others. If he does not, he may fall into the lower vibrations of Scorpio, ruthlessly seeking the material in life and ignoring others. If he follows the lower path, he is likely to fall into reckless experimentation in drugs and alcohol.

Uranus in Scorpio

Those with Uranus in Scorpio are shrewd, persistent and secretive. Aggressive and forceful, he is often rebellious. Generally, he will not accept the opinions of others. He is inventive, mechanical and often has healing abilities. If this placement is afflicted, he is prone to accidents and falls. Danger from explosives and on water is also indicated.

Neptune in Scorpio

Neptune in Scorpio lends an interest to all things metaphysical. More than likely, the native possesses mediumistic abilities and unusually sharp senses. Patient, reserved, secretive and talented, he may gain through inheritances.

Pluto in Scorpio

Natives with this placement are naturally attracted to the psychic and occult fields. During the years 1984 to1995, Pluto was transiting Scorpio. During that time, developments leading to increased longevity and improvements in birth control were made. Biological warfare loomed dangerously on the horizon.

PLANETS IN SAGITTARIUS

Sun In Sagittarius
"Expansion"

The Sun placed in the sign of Sagittarius is generous, enthusiastic, social and strives for a secure placement in life. Of a dual nature, the archer has changeable moods.

Moon in Sagittarius

Natives with their Moon falling in the sign of Sagittarius are sociable, optimistic and enthusiastic. Many public speakers are born with their Moons placed in this sign. While idealistic, their moods are changeable.

Mercury in Sagittarius

Mercury in Sagittarius indicates a person who is impulsive and versatile. Their ideas are often formed on too large a scale to be practical or carried out. Mercury in Sagittarius skips from one thing to another, often holding more than one job at a time. They are not at their best when speaking to the public as they jump from one topic to another.

Venus in Sagittarius

Venus in Sagittarius is sympathetic, kind and fun loving. Though she is generous, she is also extravagant. A romantic daydreamer, she is idealistic about love. You won't catch her home scrubbing the floors or slaving over a hot stove for she has other more refined and interesting things to do.

Mars in Sagittarius

Mars in Sagittarius is a sports fan as well as a participant. He is impulsive, enthusiastic and frank. Like Venus in Sagittarius, he is extravagant. An adventurer, he loves to travel.

Saturn in Sagittarius

Those born with Saturn in Sagittarius are often philosophical and interested in the political economy. Intuitive and prophetic, he is a humanitarian as well. Many attorneys and judges have Saturn placed in Sagittarius. If this position is not well aspected, he may become separated from his native land.

Jupiter in Sagittarius

Jupiter in Sagittarius signifies one with a noble character who has a love of justice, is religious and moral. Loyal, generous and tolerant, he is prophetic and inspirational. He enjoys helping others. More than likely, he will have interests abroad. If this position is not well aspected, he may be wasteful.

Uranus in Sagittarius

Uranus in Sagittarius is progressive, adventurous, and a risk taker. Imaginative and inventive, he has far-reaching goals in regard to reforms and is capable of carrying them out. If this position is not well aspected, he will rebel against the conventional.

Neptune in Sagittarius

This person possesses prophetic insight in regard to religion, literature and foreign affairs. He enjoys travel, is farsighted and inspiring. Many were born during 1970 through 1984 with Neptune placed in the sign of Sagittarius.

Pluto in Sagittarius

Pluto transiting Sagittarius during the years of 1995 to 2008 is expected to usher in a period of religious revival as well as transformation in the fields of education and publishing. We are already seeing this occur. Those born during these years will have an interest in pioneering advancement in these areas for what many during the late twentieth century, believed to be unattainable.

PLANETS IN CAPRICORN

"Social Foundations"
Sun in Capricorn

The Sun placed in the sign of Capricorn indicates a hardworking person. With a serious outlook on life, he clings to his goals. Tenacious, with a sense of reality, he advances in his chosen field in his dignified, diplomatic manner. If the Sun is afflicted or negatively aspected, he may be depressed, gloomy and authoritative.

Moon in Capricorn

One with their Moon placed in the sign of Capricorn will, in some way, be in the public eye. He may be prominent and well respected; however, if the Moon is not well aspected, he may ruin his reputation through lack of control of his desires. His emotions may be cold due to a disregard for others.

Mercury in Capricorn

Mercury in Capricorn has strong powers of concentration and a clear, practical, methodical mind. Though he has a wry sort of humor, he is reserved, serious, logical and is able to solve difficult problems. His view on life is serious; his driving force, ambition. He will succeed through his own merit. Many teachers and diplomats have Mercury placed in Capricorn.

Venus in Capricorn

Trustworthy, loyal, and patient, one with Venus placed in Capricorn takes a practical viewpoint on love. The native's spouse must be well-off, or at least hold a lucrative job. The danger is that the native may have too much self-control which brings separations and disappointments.

Mars in Capricorn

Mars placed in Capricorn is ambitious, independent, self-reliant, patient and deliberate. A slow learner, he assimilates knowledge. Success is important to him. If Mars in Capricorn is afflicted or poorly aspected, he is quickly irritated.

Saturn in Capricorn

Saturn in Capricorn is at home. The native who has Saturn placed in Capricorn has strong will power and concentration. Diplomatic and persistent, he may not race to the finish line, but he will achieve his goals.

Jupiter in Capricorn

Well aspected, Jupiter in Capricorn is trustworthy, correct and conscious of his goal. If afflicted or poorly aspected, he is a hypocrite. not to be trusted.

Uranus in Capricorn

Ambitious and shrewd, Uranus in Capricorn is persevering and desires to accumulate possessions. Nervous and restless, natives with Uranus in Capricorn may be domineering and have stomach and digestive problems.

Neptune in Capricorn

Intuitive, ambitious, and contemplative, natives born with Neptune in Capricorn have good business ability and make excellent researchers, artists and musicians. Meditation is an everyday practice for those born with Neptune in Capricorn. The term "supernatural" is not unfamiliar to them. They serve humanity as leaders, educators and spiritual teachers. During 1820 to 1834 and again during 1985 to 1998, many natives were born with this aspect.

Pluto in Capricorn

Pluto in Capricorn disrupts the political arena as well as authority. Those born with Pluto placed in the sign of Capricorn demand power, independence and recognition. This is the placement dictators have been born under. During the years of 2008 through 2023, Pluto will be transiting the sign of Capricorn.

PLANETS IN AQUARIUS

"Reforming"
Sun in Aquarius

The Sun in Aquarius is intuitive, adaptable, social, sympathetic and always ready to lend a helping hand. Inventive and philosophic, he is interested in science, electricity and astrology. He gains through friends and group activities.

Moon in Aquarius

Moon in Aquarius is observant, sympathetic and adaptable. She has a deep concern for others and is always ready to help. Independent and understanding, she has an abundance of progressive ideas. Unconventional, one with the Moon placed in the sign of Aquarius enjoys the unusual and what might be considered eccentric by more conservative signs. If poorly aspected, she may have a wandering life and problems through women.

Mercury in Aquarius

Mercury in Aquarius is an enthusiastic, practical and progressive thinker interested in inventions and reforms. He is witty, clever and grasps situations quickly. Well disciplined, he is able to implement his ideas. Unconcerned with others opinions, he will follow his own convictions.

Venus in Aquarius

Independent, charming and unusual, Venus in Aquarius values her freedom. She is able to remain cool, calm, and detached in most situations. She is not possessive nor is she jealous. She has contemporary views on love and requires her lover to be her friend first. This native is often born to parents who are emotionally cool and do not express their affections.

Mars in Aquarius

Intellectual, deliberate and independent, Mars in Aquarius values his freedom. Working well in groups, he enjoys implementing new techniques. A humanitarian, he is interested in reforming the masses. He is quick-witted and arrives at conclusions rapidly. Impulsive, he can be headstrong and abrupt.

Saturn in Aquarius

Reserved, courteous and affable, Saturn in Aquarius is a deep thinker. He will make a good, steady, reliable partner.

Jupiter in Aquarius

Jupiter in Aquarius is a humanitarian on a wide scale. Full of hope, with a wealth of plans, he is aware of human nature and has a sense of social justice. He is prophetic and inclined to pursue the unusual, spiritual and the mystical. His friends and acquaintances are often found among foreigners and political figures.

Uranus in Aquarius

Uranus in Aquarius is at home in this sign. Original, ingenious and intuitive, he is progressive in his beliefs and is fond of unusual pursuits. A humanitarian, he is pleasant and social. He can succeed through radio, TV, social movements and through mechanical pursuits.

Neptune in Aquarius

Natives born with Neptune placed in the sign of Aquarius are independent, enjoy nature and have unusual religious views. Expansive, they are sympathetic and humane. Neptune was transiting Aquarius during the years of 1834 to 1848 and moved into the sign of Aquarius in 1999 where it will remain until the year 2011.

Pluto in Aquarius

From 1777 to1799, Pluto was transiting the sign of Aquarius. During that time, there was a period of humanitarian reform. Important astronomical and electrical discoveries were made. Natives born with Pluto transiting Aquarius were well liked, with a wealth of plans and an urge to reform. They advanced through life with the help of others.

PLANETS IN PISCES

"I Feel"
Sun in Pisces

Sun in Pisces is secretive, reserved, moody, sensitive, honest and kind to those in distress. He or she is idealistic, inspirational, and possesses psychic and mediumistic qualities, but lacks confidence and is timid.

Moon in Pisces

Optimistic, quiet, sympathetic, fond of beauty and harmony, one with their Moon in the sign of Pisces is apt to become easily discouraged. She has problems with saving money, is often misunderstood and does not have stable love relationships. She enjoys reading, especially romance novels.

Mercury in Pisces

One with Mercury placed in the water sign of Pisces is imaginative, receptive, intuitive and telepathic. If this position is negatively aspected, the native may live in the past; trapped by his memories. He may be shy, live a secluded life, and daydream his time away.

Venus in Pisces

Venus in Pisces has a carefree nature; is impressionable and enjoys art, music, beauty, and nature. Sensitive and psychic, Venus in Pisces may be fickle in love and have more than one marriage.

Mars in Pisces

Mars in Pisces works alone while he hopes and waits for success. He is quiet and easily becomes depressed due to vacillation, yet he accomplishes much. Sympathetic and affectionate, he is generous with his money. Interested in the occult, he tends to join secret organizations. He may find success working as a sea captain, a fisherman, or an investigator.

Saturn in Pisces

Saturn in Pisces is modest, reserved and timid. He performs difficult work quietly, by himself yet, he is ingenious and aspiring . His health is often affected by psychic conditions with colds and lingering illnesses. He suffers from depression and loneliness but may improve through psychic research or institutions.

Jupiter in Pisces

One with Jupiter placed in the water sign of Pisces is content, kindhearted, and enjoys solitude. Compassionate, he enjoys working in hospitals. Unassuming, Jupiter in Pisces may benefit through psychic research. If this position is afflicted, he may lose through deception.

Uranus in Pisces

Uranus was transiting the sign of Pisces from 1836 through 1844 and again during 1919 through 1928. Uranus entered Pisces once again for a brief period of time during 2003. Taking a retrograde position, it returned to the sign of Aquarius until Dec. 31, 2003 when the planet once again entered Pisces for a long stay. It will remain in Pisces until March of 2011. Children born during this time will be unusual, fond of the occult and psychic research. Many will experience visions and have precognitive dreams.

Neptune in Pisces

During the years of 1847 to 1862, Neptune was transiting the sign of Pisces. Children born during those years were reserved, sympathetic, and charitable. Inclined to mysticism and artistic pursuits, they had a love of the sea and travel by water. In 2012, Neptune will once again enter the sign of Pisces until 2026.

Pluto in Pisces

Pluto in Pisces, during the years of 1799 to 1822, ushered in a period of emphasis on mystical and psychic phenomenon. A romantic interest in the fine arts, music, religion and philosophy flared. Methods of treating the mentally ill and retarded were improved upon as well as care for the homeless and aged. New methods of nursing flourished.

Questionnaire

1. What sign is impulsive, courageous, quick tempered, and willful?

2. Would you hire an employee with Moon in Aries based on his/her ability to complete tasks?

3. Describe Mercury in Aries.

4. When placed in Aries, is Venus in her exaltation?

5. Is one with Venus placed in Aries a good bet for marriage?

6. Is Jupiter in Aries known to benefit from legal matters or the law?

7. What sign describes "I am?"

8. What sign describes "I have?"

9. Describe one with Moon in Taurus.

10. Describe Mars in Aries.

11. What sign describes "I think?"

12. Does Gemini have stable moods?

13. Describe Gemini.

14. Describe Sun in Cancer.

15. Is one with his or her Moon in Cancer family oriented?

16. Sensitive?

17. What planet or light, when falling in Cancer causes the native stomach problems of indigestion?

18. "I will" describes what zodiac sign?

19. "The Mistress of Love" or "Society's Queen" has her Moon in what sign?

20. From what ailment may Mars in Leo suffer?

21. What sign describes one who says "I analyze?"

22. What sign describes one who is shy, reserved, diligent, yet a perfectionist and a worrier?

23. What sign describes "I balance"?

24. Describe Libra.

25. "Involvement" describes what sign?"

26. Is one with Venus in Scorpio jealous?

27. What is her lesson?

28. What sign describes "With passion!"

29. Describe Venus in Sagittarius.

30. Describe one with Sun in Capricorn.

31. Is one with Mars in Capricorn ambitious?

32. Describe Mercury in Aquarius.

33. Is Mars in Aquarius a humanitarian?

34. Describe Sun in Pisces.

35. Describe Venus in Pisces. Do you think she might be fickle in love?

Chapter 5

THE HOUSES

The First House

The first house, an angular house and the natural house of Aries, is ruled by Mars. It represents the personality, the head and the face. A planet falling in an angular house such as the first, the fourth, seventh and tenth is said to be "accidentally dignified." Because of its placement, the planets are strengthened.

When a planet falls in the first house, look to the house it rules. For example, if Venus falls into your first house and rules the seventh house, partnership affairs will play an important part in your life. Now look to the ruler of the first house. If the ruler is Mars (Aries ascendant), and falls into your fifth house of speculation, children, love affairs and entertainment, this is how your ascendant may best be expressed.

The Second House

The second house, the natural house of Taurus is ruled by Venus. It represents financial matters and is a succedent house. Planets are not strengthened nor are they weakened when they fall into this house. The parts of the body the second house represents are the throat and ears.

The Third House

The third house, the natural house of Gemini, is ruled by Mercury. It is a cadent house, representing short trips, writings, and mental abilities. It also represents the shoulders, collarbones, arms, hands, and the nervous system. Planets falling into the cadent houses are said to be weakened or accidentally debilitated except for the natural rulers of the cadent houses.

The Fourth House

The fourth house, the natural house of Cancer, is ruled by the Moon. It is an angular house representing the home, the environment, the father and the conditions at the close of life. This house rules the breast, stomach and digestive tract. Since it is an angular house, planets falling into this house are said to be strengthened.

The Fifth House

The fifth house, the natural house of Leo, is ruled by the Sun. A succedent house, the planets are neither strengthened nor are they weakened when placed in this position. Romance, matters of the heart, speculation, entertainment, children, circulation, vitality and the heart are ruled by the fifth house. If many planets fall into the fifth, the native may work with children but may not have them himself. If a malefic planet is located in this house, the native may have problems raising a child.

The Sixth House

The sixth house, a cadent house and the natural house of Virgo, is ruled by Mercury. Because it is a cadent house, the planets are weakened when falling into this house except for its ruler, Mercury. Matters of health, service, work, small animals, employees, restaurants, groceries and clothing are ruled by this house as well as the health, solar plexus and bowels.

The Seventh House

The seventh house, the natural house of Libra, is ruled by Venus. It is an angular house that indicates that the planets falling into this house are strengthened. It represents partnerships, marriage, the public, lawsuits, open enemies, the kidneys, lower back, and the ovaries. The cusp of the seventh house is referred to as the descendant and describes the partner or the partner's qualities. More than likely, the native does not have these qualities himself. The seventh house also indicates the native's purpose or destiny this lifetime. For example, if the seventh house cusp is a fixed sign (Taurus, Scorpio, Leo, or Aquarius) the native will not want a divorce. Note the ruler of the seventh house. Where is it placed? Its placement will tell you where you will meet your mate.

The Eighth House

The eighth house, natural house of Scorpio, is ruled by Pluto. It is a succedent house in which no planet is either strengthened nor is it weakened. The eighth house rules money of others, legacies, astral experiences, financial affairs of the partner, the muscular system, bladder, and reproductive organs.

The Ninth House

The ninth house, the natural house of Sagittarius, is ruled by Jupiter and is a cadent house. All planets, with the exception of its ruler are weakened when placed in this position. The ninth house rules long journeys; higher education, publishing, philanthropic, philosophical, and spiritual affairs as well as the liver and thighs.

The Tenth House

The tenth house, the natural home of Capricorn, is ruled by Saturn. It is an angular house in which all planets are strengthened when falling into this house. The tenth house rules the career, employer, the mother, honor, fame, promotion, affairs of the country, and the knees. While the next house, the eleventh, is the house of hopes and wishes, it is the tenth house that tells us what actually exists.

The Eleventh House

The eleventh house, the natural home of Aquarius, is ruled by Uranus and is a succedent house. Planets placed in this house are neither strengthened nor are they weakened. This house rules friends, associations, hopes and wishes, the financial condition of the employer and the ankles.

The Twelfth House

The twelfth house, the natural home of Pisces, is ruled by Neptune. A cadent house, all planets are weakened, except for its ruler, when placed in this house. The twelfth house represents self-undoing, secret sorrows, limitations, seclusion, secret enemies, hospitals, large animals, the occult and the feet. When a planet falls in the twelfth house, look to the house of the ruler. That is the area of the native's life that there may be problems. For instance, if Aries is on the twelfth house cusp, look to see where Mars, the ruler of the twelfth house cusp falls. If it falls in the second house, your problems will be with money; the fifth house, with children and speculation.

NOTE:

In transit, if Mars is retrograde and conjunct with the seventh house cusp, the native's marriage will not occur. Someone is likely to cancel the engagement and back out of the forthcoming union.

Chapter 6

THE PLANETS IN THE HOUSES

Sun in the First House

The Sun placed in the first house lends an Aries connotation to the individual. Courageous, enthusiastic and bold with a tendency to be hasty, he is an innovator with a strong nature. Passionate in his beliefs, he may be ruthless. If the Sun is well aspected, good health is indicated.

Sun in the Second House

An individual whose Sun is placed in his second house, is persevering, practical and steadfast. He is likely to be possessive of things and people. Desiring security, he seeks to obtain it through acquiring possessions and material items. Generous, ambitious, with a fine sense of humor, he seeks pleasure and enjoyment.

Sun in the Third House

Creative and self-reliant, a native with his Sun placed in the third house is curious and versatile with a desire to learn. Vivacious, adaptable and restless, he loves change.

Sun in the Fourth House

The Sun in the fourth house re-acts just as the Sun placed in Cancer would. He is receptive, reserved, domestic, loves the institution of marriage and family-life. Conservative, experiencing many of life's ups and downs, he tends to retreat during difficult times.

Sun in the Fifth House

The Sun placed in the fifth house is creative, enjoys life and is often a risk taker. You will often find one with their Sun placed in the fifth house in the fields of sports and acting. They are happiest when creating and giving joy to others.

Sun in the Sixth House

The Sun placed in the sixth house is orderly, methodical, and analytical, much as a Virgo is. They enjoy being of service to others, pleasing them and taking pride in their accomplishments. Although they have good re-cooperative powers, they are often worry warts and fault-finders.

Sun in the Seventh House

One with his Sun placed in the seventh house possesses fine manners, a love of the arts and desires harmony. Sociable, he longs to be important. Associations are important to him, but he lacks consistency and an ability to make a firm decision within a reasonable amount of time.

Sun in the Eighth House

A person whose Sun is placed in the eighth house is tenacious, passionate and fearless. He has a great deal of willpower and strives for improvement. Usually, his finances are stable and he may inherit money and possessions. He is naturally drawn to the mystic, the occult and to the psychic realms.

Sun in the Ninth House

With his Sun placed in the ninth house, the native is a natural philosopher, has high ideals and a respect for others opinions. Generous and sociable, he seeks the truth and possesses a strong aptitude for languages and a desire to travel.

Sun in the Tenth House

A native whose Sun is placed in the tenth house seeks success and power. His strongest motivation is to succeed in a career. Hard working, with a serious outlook on life, he is tenacious and realistic.

Sun in the Eleventh House

The Sun placed in the eleventh house indicates that the native has an intuitive understanding of others. He is observant, adaptable, and is always ready to lend a helping hand. Sympathetic, he rises in life through his own efforts but receives well deserved help from others. A humanitarian, he has a wide range of friends, enjoys working with groups, and is responsible, broad-minded and liberal.

Sun in the Twelfth House

One with their Sun placed in the twelfth house is reserved, receptive, moody and secretive. They often suffer from restrictions that have been caused through inhibitions and negative attitudes. Preferring to retreat from society, they are empathetic with sick and mentally ill people. Oftentimes, they possess clairvoyant and psychic powers. Though they lack confidence in their abilities, they may become excellent doctors and nurses.

When the natal Sun falls into the twelfth house, the house of self-undoing and hidden secrets, count the degrees from the Sun to the degree of the ascending sign. The number of degrees will indicate the number of years the native will have financial difficulties in his early life. As the Sun progresses into his first and second house, the native's finances will generally improve unless other indications in the chart contradict this.

The Moon in the First House

Strongly influenced by his early life and by his mother, the Moon placed in his first house indicates a native who is restless, impulsive and super sensitive to his environment. Though he may wish his life to be different, he may lack the courage to change it. If the Moon is conjunct the first house cusp or the ascendant, there is an indication there may have been problems at birth.

The Moon in the Second House

Natives with the Moon placed in their second house appreciate beauty and enjoy life. Their desire to accumulate material goods and wealth is for their own emotional security.

The Moon in the Third House

The Moon in the third house gives many hopes, wishes and interests. The native is susceptible to environmental influences and may fall quickly into despondency. Disliking routine of any kind, they are adaptable and curious, interested in learning by listening rather than by studying.

The Moon in the Fourth House

The Moon placed in the native's fourth house is domestic, economical and needs peace and security. Intuitive, impressionable and affectionate, he is interested in family matters. His mother will be of great influence to him, one way or another. Many changes of residency or at least of continual redecoration are indicated by this placement. Tension may result in stomach problems.

The Moon in the Fifth House

The native with his Moon placed in his fifth house is charming and enjoys being the center of attention. He is intuitive, self-confident and generous. A social creature, he seeks pleasure, is affectionate with his children and enjoys luxury. Afflicted, he may be snobbish, vain and overestimate himself. He must control his fluctuating emotions or his creativity may be hindered.

The Moon in the Sixth House

The Moon placed in the sixth house indicates one who will enjoy employment in the service fields. He is most interested in health and diet. As far as love and marriage go, his head rules his heart and he has a practical approach on life. Methodical, he loves tidiness, proper behavior and simplicity.

The Moon in the Seventh House

The Moon placed in the seventh house indicates a native who requires a lively social life as well as love and affection. He or she is dependent upon his partner. If this position is afflicted, he will be self-indulgent and interested in trivial matters.

The Moon in the Eighth House

One who has his Moon placed in the eighth house will gain financially through business, his marriage partner or through inheritance on his mother's side. His or her partner is likely to be moody or overly sensitive. The native may be psychic, interested in the occult, ruthless, frank, ambitious and overestimate himself.

The Moon in the Ninth House

The Moon placed in the ninth house indicates a native who enjoys new experiences that add to his or her philosophy of life. Interested in sports, hobbies, and learning, he or may become an excellent teacher. This person is one who is always searching for "greener pastures" because he is never content with life as it is.

The Moon in the Tenth House

One with their Moon placed in the tenth house has a special charisma and may work with the public. They are ambitious and may tend to change occupations often. Patient and tenacious, they have a practical outlook on life.

The Moon in the Eleventh House

A native whose Moon is placed in the eleventh house works for the group rather than himself. He has many friends, is sympathetic, adaptable, and enjoys helping others.

The Moon in the Twelfth House

A native with his or her Moon placed in the twelfth house is moody and has hidden sorrows others are not aware of. This person lacks self-confidence and needs to help others avoid the pitfalls and sorrows they have suffered.

Mercury in the First House

Mercury, when placed in the first house, indicates one who is adaptable, eloquent and humorous. The native's thinking is creative. Mentally active, he or she is observant, enthusiastic and quick. His lectures and writings reflect his own opinions or experiences. Mercury falling in the first house indicates that the native's nerves are on edge. Because of it, he or she will be slender. Meditation and chamomile tea would be calming for this native.

Mercury in the Second House

Logical, deliberate, quick-witted and versatile, a native with Mercury falling into the second house is motivated toward making money. He or she is able to communicate well through writing or speaking. Listening to music and reading are sources of pleasure.

Mercury in the Third House

His mind is quick and perceptive. He is interested in literature, science and current affairs. Speaking, writing and lecturing come easy to one with Mercury in the third house. Fond of studying, reading, writing and traveling, he is interested in his relatives and neighbors.

Mercury in the Fourth House

Perceptive, with a good memory, the native who has Mercury in the fourth house is studious and enjoys studying at home. He is high strung and may change residences many times.

Mercury in the Fifth House

Creative and enthusiastic, the native whose Mercury falls into the fifth house is farsighted with many plans. He enjoys speculation, entertainment, and travel.

Mercury in the Sixth House

Tidy, practical and patient, this native is interested in hygiene, holistic health and medicine. One with Mercury falling in his sixth house may gain through his writings, particularly on subjects he is interested in.

Mercury in the Seventh House

Adaptable, with a sense of justice, Mercury in the seventh house makes a good teammate in business. The native's marriage may be unsettling to him for it is more of a marriage of the mind than of the senses. The native is tactful, with a sense of form and beauty.

Mercury in the Eighth House

A native whose Mercury is placed in the eighth house is interested in the occult and life after death. He may be able to communicate through automatic writing with those who have passed on. This position indicates one who has a talent for research and analysis.

Mercury in the Ninth House

This position of Mercury indicates a native who is philosophical, with many interests. Striving for justice and the truth, he is capable of expressing his beliefs verbally. Learning a foreign language is a "natural" for this native. He will take the easiest route, evading difficulties. On the negative side, he is likely to scatter his energies.

Mercury in the Tenth House

Patient, logical, with good powers of concentration, this native views life on the serious side. He is ambitious, economical, and will succeed on his own merit. This position indicates writing and speaking abilities. If negatively aspected, he may become melancholy and cunning.

Mercury in the Eleventh House

Adaptable and intellectual, the native with Mercury falling in his eleventh house prefers friends who stimulate his mind. He enjoys others who have opposing interests. A progressive thinker, he is interested in inventions and reforms.

Mercury in the Twelfth House

A native whose Mercury falls in the twelfth house may be easily influenced by others and lack self-confidence. Receptive, imaginative, and intuitive, he is interested in metaphysical subjects. He or she is secretive and able to analyze others problems. Though they may be misunderstood by relatives, they make excellent psychologists.

Venus in the First House

Attractive, friendly, and magnetic, Venus in the first house receives benefits and has the ability to receive what she wants in life. He or she is a romantic dreamer and believes in love at first sight. Negatively aspected, he or she may be selfish.

Venus in the Second House

Venus in the second house is faithful, conservative, loves luxury and precious gemstones. Money comes easily to the native with Venus located in the second house. It may be gained through marriage, jewelry, hotels, apparel, artistic or musical pursuits. Much of his or her money is spent on luxury items, friends and social pursuits.

Venus in the Third House

Cheerful, optimistic and peaceful, a native with Venus in the third house enjoys the arts, music, opera, and literature. She is charming, courteous and cooperative. On the negative side, she may have shallow or superficial love interests that lead to conflicts.

Venus in the Fourth House

A person whose Venus falls into the fourth house enjoys family, home, art and music. They may gain through inheritance, property or investments. He or she must not eat too many sweets or delicacies, or digestive problems may occur.

Venus in the Fifth House

One with Venus in the fifth house dresses well and enjoys a life of luxury. This person gains through children, love affairs and friendships. He or she entertains others well and achieves success through social ties, pleasure, amusements and speculation. If Venus is poorly aspected, his health suffers from overindulgence and through unwise love affairs. If this position is poorly aspected by Saturn, the native may suffer through love, speculation, and children.

Venus in the Sixth House

Venus in the sixth house is moral and practical in her love affairs. She is diplomatic and well liked by fellow workers. She may find success in the fields of nursing, hygiene, pets, and clothing. Sugars and starches should be avoided.

Venus in the Seventh House

Friendly, with good taste and fine manners, a person with Venus falling in the seventh house is often artistic. If Venus is well placed in the seventh house, she may marry early. Afflicted, there may be sorrow and loss through marriage.

Venus in the Eighth House

One with Venus placed in the eighth house has strong powers of attraction. He or she is passionate, jealous and has a tendency to waste his or her energies. The native may lack self-discipline and be lazy. He or she is likely to inherit money; however, there may be problems obtaining it.

Venus in the Ninth House

A native with Venus falling in their ninth house is idealistic, hypersensitive, diplomatic, kind, enjoys travel and may relocate far away from his or her birth place.

Venus in the Tenth House

Friendly, optimistic, responsible and faithful, this person may tend to gravitate toward more mature partners. This position indicates self-control in love relationships. Venus in the tenth house often bestows a lovely voice favorable for both singing and public speaking.

Venus in the Eleventh House

One with their Venus placed in the eleventh house has contemporary views toward love relationships. They are independent, tactful and friendly.

Venus in the Twelfth House

A native with Venus placed in their twelfth house has a strong sense of compassion and desires to serve others. This person is interested in seeking the meaning of life. He or she prefers to keep their love relationships secret as well as his or her innermost feelings.

Mars in the First House

At home in this house, Mars is independent, courageous and loves his freedom. Ambitious, confident, and enterprising, the native may be reckless, going where angels fear to tread. Headstrong, he may be impatient. Much depends upon the sign of this house. Afflicted, there is a danger of head injuries and many arguments.

Mars in the Second House

One with Mars placed in their second house works diligently to acquire money and possessions. He or she is efficient and may gain through stock farming, chemicals, timber, working in sales or as a promoter. This person may be overly generous and careless with money if Mars is poorly aspected.

Mars in the Third House

Energetic, with a sharp mind, one with Mars falling in the third house is enthusiastic and determined. He is analytical and quick to speak. Mars falling into the third house indicates arguments with brothers and sisters in his childhood. Nervous and high-strung, his speech may be biting or sarcastic, especially if Mars is negatively aspected.

Mars in the Fourth House

Independent, a person with Mars falling in the fourth house may leave home early to establish a home of his own. He is impulsive, moody, lacks perseverance and self-control.

Mars in the Fifth House

Mars in the fifth house is self-confident, self-assured, creative, enterprising and responsible. On the negative side, he may gamble, be an egotist and have problems with his children.

Mars in the Sixth House

Mars in the sixth house is methodical, enjoys detail and has a love of tidiness. Efficient and dynamic, he is critical to others who do not have those qualities. Mechanically minded, he is industrious. This position of Mars is similar to a Mars- Mercury conjunction and indicates fevers when ill.

Mars in the Seventh House

Mars in the seventh house is friendly, cordial and social. Enthusiastic, he is focused upon partnerships. He must cultivate harmony and diplomacy.

Mars in the Eighth House

Mars in the eighth house is ambitious, critical and excellent at research. Goal oriented and ruthless, he is a survivalist. This position may indicate difficulties regarding deceased persons and financial loss through an extravagant partner.

Mars in the Ninth House

Mars in the ninth house is frank, enthusiastic, enjoys sports, competition and freedom of thought. There may be problems through religious or legal matters. A danger of violence in foreign lands, problems with long trips and with the partner's relatives may exist. If not well aspected, the native may be rash, extravagant, and crave adventure.

Mars in the Tenth House

Mars in the tenth house is ambitious, realistic, independent, and deliberate. He is courageous, energetic and resourceful and will do well being in business for himself. If well aspected, he will gain by the father or by inheritance.

Mars in the Eleventh House

Mars in the eleventh house has many acquaintances, is good at organization and has a love of freedom. He is capable of social leadership but needs to learn to say no more often.

Mars in the Twelfth House

Mars in the twelfth house works silently and struggles for recognition. Intensely emotional, feeling a great sense of aloneness, he or she has repressed desires. It is necessary for this native to overcome inner resentments. Unless well aspected, he or she may have addictions and a lack of self-control. Slander, loss of reputation, and treachery are possible as well as imprisonment.

Jupiter in the First House

Jupiter in the first house indicates one who is honest, noble, generous, assertive and has the capability for leadership. There may be a problem with being overly optimistic. Because Jupiter signifies expansion, Jupiter placed in the first house or on the ascendant may indicate a problem with weight gain.

Jupiter in the Second House

Jupiter in the second house is offered an opportunity for wealth in regard to government and business affairs, law, banking, religion, science, literature, publishing, and travel, especially to foreign lands . He is confident and optimistic with visionary ideas. If negatively aspected, he may be over-extravagant.

Jupiter in the Third House

Jupiter in the third house has good manners; enjoys change; has many acquaintances, and is optimistic, philosophical, and intuitive. The natives are well liked and are often successful in literature, publishing, traveling, teaching, or speaking. If this position is poorly aspected, they may be mentally restless and scatter their energies.

Jupiter in the Fourth House

This position is favorable for the native's family and home life. Gain will be through the parents, land and possessions. Success comes later in life as well as a probable inheritance. One with Jupiter falling in his fourth house is generous, and hospitable.

Jupiter in the Fifth House

Jupiter in the fifth house is creative and sympathetic but may have a tendency to gamble. He or she is self-confident and enjoys luxury. It is a good position for a popular leader.

Jupiter in the Sixth House

Jupiter in the sixth house is ambitious, dependable, ethical, and moral. One with this placement generally has good health and would make an excellent teacher.

Jupiter in the Seventh House

One who has Jupiter placed in the seventh house generally will benefit financially through marriage and partnerships. They are social; good natured, and more than likely will have a successful marriage perhaps, followed by a second.

Jupiter in the Eighth House

Jupiter in the eighth house is emotional and has psychic abilities which may be used to benefit others. He is likely to gain through inheritances. One with Jupiter placed in the eighth house is optimistic but ruthless in pursuing material goods and possessions.

Jupiter in the Ninth House

Philosophical, religious and prophetic, Jupiter in the ninth house represents a native who is intuitive, tolerant and has good judgment. He will benefit through traveling, especially to foreign lands. His accomplishments may not be recognized until the latter part of his life.

Jupiter in the Tenth House

Jupiter in the tenth house possesses qualities of leadership and focuses on the goals he has set. He is trustworthy, responsible, and charismatic. On the negative side, he may be an egotist and a hypocrite.

Jupiter in the Eleventh House

One who has Jupiter placed in the eleventh house is a humanitarian, social and well liked. He or she has the ability to succeed in group activities.

Jupiter in the Twelfth House

Jupiter in the twelfth house is content in modest circumstances, enjoys solitude, and works quietly and successfully behind the scenes. Kind, with a desire to help others, he is a philanthropist. On the negative side, he is impressionable and enjoys alcohol and tobacco products. He may be unrealistic and must think through his plans carefully.

Saturn in the First House

Saturn placed in the first house is modest, reserved, faithful, and serious. Industrious, self-controlled, and ambitious, they will go their own way alone, if necessary. Easily depressed, they may suffer from a feeling of not being loved in their childhood. These natives will encounter many problems, responsibilities, and obstacles in life. Progress and success will be slow, but through persistence, honor and credit will be gained. They need to accomplish and are thoughtful and considerate of others. One with Saturn on their ascendant or placed in their first house will bruise easily. They may need more vitamin supplements than usual and suffer from malnutrition. St. John's Wort might help lift this native's spirit. When Saturn is transiting the first house, the native may lose weight.

Saturn in the Second House

One with Saturn in the second house worries about his or her possessions and must learn to share with others. They are thrifty, practical, responsible, and must persevere to make money. The opportunity for success lies with land, property, investments, or through the employer.

Saturn in the Third House

This person is thorough, conscientious, and logical. He will learn all his life. Saturn in the third indicates the possibility of delays and disappointments in regard to his or her education, writings, relatives, neighbors, and short trips. He or she may have a gloomy attitude and become lonely because he unconsciously fears disappointments.

Saturn in the Fourth House

This placement of Saturn indicates many problems and responsibilities at home. His or her mother is a strong influence in his or her life, either for good or bad, depending upon the aspects. One with Saturn placed in his fourth house is reserved, but has a love for independence.

Saturn in the Fifth House

Saturn placed in a native's fifth house indicates one who is loyal, cautious, reliable, but shy, especially in social situations. This position indicates a loss of a child or trouble and unhappiness because of them.

They may feel that their children are a burden and will not understand them. The native is emotionally and creatively restricted, appearing distant to others, including their children. In love affairs, this native will prefer an older partner. The placement of Saturn in this house indicates that there will be disappointments or delays in love. It is not wise for this native to speculate or gamble for this placement indicates loss by these things.

Saturn in the Sixth House

Serious, thorough and responsible, Saturn in the sixth house is discreet. The native is likely to have many illnesses and lost opportunities through his poor health. This is not a good position for employment or pets.

Saturn in the Seventh House

One with Saturn placed in his seventh house is loyal, with a strong sense of duty. This native is extremely sensitive and cautious about marriage. He may marry for security rather than love and will not leave his mate even if the union is unsuccessful.

Note: Astrologers should double check their calculations. Oftentimes, when Saturn falls in a native's seventh house, it is an indication that the chart has not been calculated correctly.

Saturn in the Eighth House

Obstinate, a diligent worker with a serious outlook on life, one with Saturn placed in his eighth house is patient and self-disciplined. In his quest for security through monetary gain, he must not forget to relate to others in partnerships and groups. It is in this way that he will gain wisdom and understanding of others.

Saturn in the Ninth House

This position produces excellent teachers and public speakers. These natives are studious, meditative, prudent, are capable of deep concentration. They are honest, just and interested in philosophy and religion.

Saturn in the Tenth House

Saturn in the tenth house is capable of deep concentration, self-restraint, and endurance The natives are strong-willed, economical, and diplomatic. Advancement in life is slow but sure. They have good business ability but may be egotistical. If so, they must develop humility. Because Saturn is placed in the tenth house of the father or dominant parent, this signifies that there was a lack of a father image. Perhaps he died while the native was young, or maybe the parents were divorced or the father was cold and distant to his children.

Saturn in the Eleventh House

This position indicates that the native has a reliable partner. He or she participates in group interests for serious reasons rather than for pleasure or recreation. Though the native may perform services for the group, he or she will not receive recognition due him. Many contacts are indicated but few friends.

Saturn in the Twelfth

Saturn in the twelfth indicates a sensitive, modest and reserved person. He or she lacks self-confidence, is shy, and works alone in seclusion often with no recognition.

Uranus in the First House

Uranus placed in the first house indicates a native who has a love of freedom, is independent and enthusiastic. Interested in the occult, they have metaphysical ability and are attracted to astrology, psychic research, telepathy and hypnotism. Often, these natives have an inventive genius. To the more conservative types, they may appear eccentric and ahead of their time. This placement indicates many changes in residence and occupations. Marriage usually brings difficulties and separations. There is danger through lightning, electricity, machinery, explosives and airplanes. If Uranus is conjunct with the first house cusp, the ascendant, this indicates that the birth was premature. If the natal Moon is conjunct the first house cusp, this indicates there were problems at birth.

Uranus in the Second House

Uranus in the second house has an unusual way of earning money. These people are resourceful and aren't dominated by monetary or material goods. This position indicates fluctuation in income; however, the native has the ability to extricate himself from financial reversals. He is independent, inventive and values money for the freedom it offers them to pursue their talents.

Uranus in the Third House

This native has an inventive and curious mind. Mentally restless, he changes his mind often. It is a good position for writers and speakers. He or she is a good organizer, enjoys traveling to unusual places and has the ability to be clairvoyant and telepathic. One with Uranus in the third house is capable of magnetic healing. He is interested in unusual and ancient studies such as astrology and the occult.

Uranus in the Fourth House

Uranus in the fourth house has many changes in his home, domestic disruptions, problems with family affairs and may be separated from his parents. His career is often interrupted and he may suddenly be stricken with poverty. If an inheritance is expected, it is often lost.

Uranus in the Fifth House

Uranus in the fifth house is creative, original, independent and prefers unusual entertainment. The native's children will be unusual. This person has secret and impulsive love affairs that may possibly result in a scandal or social disgrace. The native may lose his first child possibly through separation. A woman with Uranus placed in her fifth house may have problems in childbirth. Speculation is not advised.

Uranus in the Sixth House

Uranus in the sixth house has unique methods of work and a good mind with unique ideas. They are nervous and may have unusual accidents in the workplace. They prefer to be their own boss or at least work irregular hours. Holistic medicine, psychic healing, magnetic healing, and herbal treatments are most successful for the native with Uranus in the sixth house. This person would succeed as a metaphysician or an electrician.

Uranus in the Seventh House

Uranus in the seventh house is romantic, inspiring, artistic, creative and may have an unusual musical talent. His views on marriage are unusual. He or she is apt to have several partnerships or marriages, and his spouse is apt to be most unusual.

Uranus in the Eighth House

Energetic and forceful, this native can be ruthless. Intuitive and psychic, he or she has unusual ideas about life, death, and sex. This native has a quick temper and nervous tension. Gain through unusual sources or an unexpected inheritance is indicated.

Uranus in the Ninth House

Uranus in the ninth house has an unusual mind, is independent, intuitive and enjoys studying metaphysics and taking unexpected trips. He may experience prophetic dreams, prophecies, and visions. This person is adventurous and rebels against tradition.

Uranus in the Tenth House

Uranus in the tenth House is independent, ambitious, and able to concentrate upon his unusual goals. A humanitarian, he or she is also interested in all things metaphysical. Many changes are indicated in this native's career.

Uranus in the Eleventh House

Uranus in the eleventh house is a humanitarian with unusual ideas. This native has unusual or eccentric friends and contacts. He or she may belong to unusual groups and may change goals often. On the negative side, he may be rebellious and guilty of exaggeration.

Uranus in the Twelfth House

Uranus in the twelfth house indicates a person who is rarely understood due to his secretive nature. A lonely person, he is interested in metaphysics and has unusual psychic experiences. This native must learn to live in the "now." Well aspected, he may have unusual success in intuitions. Afflicted, he may be violent due to psychic disturbances and placed in institutions.

Neptune in the First House

Receptive, imaginative, and mediumistic, this native will assume the conditions of the environment and of those he associates with. The native may be attracted to the psychic realms and mysterious places. Warning: The native must beware of drugs, gases, medicines, alcohol, and séances.

Neptune in the Second House

One whose Neptune is placed in the second house is creative, tactful, imaginative, intuitive and psychic. These people may be quite generous or if Neptune is poorly aspected, dishonest. Neptune in the second house is vulnerable to theft, fraudulent schemes and deception.

Neptune in the Third House

One who has Neptune placed in their third house is intuitive, inspirational, and often clairvoyant. These people have a vivid imagination, are impressionable and enjoy nature. More than likely, their memories are cloudy and they may have had feelings of insecurity in their childhood. Their psychic gifts need to be focused in the right direction; otherwise, they could suffer from obsessions or hallucinations.

Neptune in the Fourth House

Sensitive and affectionate, natives with Neptune placed in the fourth house idealizes his home environment. A native with this placement is often adopted or may become a recluse.

Neptune in the Fifth House

Creative and imaginative, many entertainers have Neptune placed in their fifth house. Natives with this placement may suffer from frustrating love affairs. One of the native's children may suffer from ill health and need special care.

Neptune in the Sixth House

Idealistic, inspirational, and humanitarian, this native may have problems focusing on details. They are sensitive and may suffer from cruelty from others in the workplace. Herbal remedies and holistic health procedures are recommended for this native. This person should avoid narcotics, opiates and clothing worn by another. He should not eat food received from one who is ill. Many vegetarians have Neptune in the sixth house. It is the healthiest food for the native. He is extraordinarily sensitive to his environment and has the ability to develop psychometrizing powers.

Neptune in the Seventh House

One with Neptune placed in their seventh house is apt to search for the ideal partner. He is not likely to find this because he must learn to be tolerant and compassionate in order to receive cooperation. If he marries, his partner may be deceptive, ill, or die. This is not a good position for partnership matters unless it is well aspected. It is the position of one who has a platonic love.

Neptune in the Eighth House

This native has the ability to communicate with those who have passed on. He has unusual dreams and psychic experiences. Participating in séances and investigating metaphysical subjects may be of great interest to him. If this position is afflicted, there may be money problems after his marriage and fraud or deceit in regard to inheritances.

Neptune in the Ninth House

One with Neptune placed in his ninth house is inspirational and may have an overactive imagination. They are philosophic and religious but exaggerate. They do not often think their plans through. If this is afflicted, there could be problems with voyages over water, legal affairs, and in-laws.

Neptune in the Tenth House

Inspirational, idealistic and humanitarian, this native may achieve honors in an artistic or scientific field. He or she may gain from liquids, hospitals, the sea or metaphysics. The native may also gain through spiritual or metaphysical friends. If this position is afflicted, there may be an unusual career, possibly connected with a scandal, and separation from the parents. Neptune falling into the tenth house may indicate a chart that is difficult to interpret, or perhaps the astrologer has miscalculated or misinterpreted the horoscope.

Neptune in the Eleventh House

One with Neptune placed in their eleventh house has noble ambitions. He may have friends who are poets, musicians, psychics, swimmers, yachtsmen and bartenders. Afflicted, there may be deceit from friends.

Neptune in the Twelfth House

Psychic, intuitive, and reserved, this person has strong feelings of loneliness and of being bound to another. The native is compassionate and may be of service to others. Many doctors and nurses have Neptune placed in their twelfth house.

Pluto in the First House

A native whose Pluto falls in his first house has extraordinary powers of leadership. Often a loner, he thinks of himself as unique. Courageous, with a strong will, these natives are magnetic, gentle, and sensitive, but may become outraged when upset. Ruled by near-uncontrollable subconscious drives, he desires personal power. Secretive, this native surrounds himself with an aura of mystery.

Pluto in the Second House

A native whose Pluto falls in the second house desires money, possessions and property. He has good judgment and financial ability but needs to learn to share with others. This native desires to restore order out of chaos. If negatively aspected, the native must be coaxed into working for his or her livelihood.

Pluto in the Third House

One who has Pluto placed in the third house is visionary, psychic, versatile, inquisitive, inspired, and searches for the meaning of life. This is a good position for a scientist, lecturer or an adventurer for he or she is enjoys change.

Pluto in the Fourth House

This native has a good imagination, is intuitive, contemplative and good at research. This is the position of the magician. Pluto placed in one's fourth house also indicates that his or her mother was a strong influence in his or her life. This native desires to explore the world, is a restless wanderer and is not fit for daily routine. A word of warning: Due to strong inner tensions, he or she has an explosive temper.

Pluto in the Fifth House

One who has Pluto placed in the fifth house is burdened with heavy responsibilities with his children. He is creative and unusually talented. On the negative side, he is prone to gambling, speculation and is inclined to have secret love affairs.

Pluto in the Sixth House

Pluto in the sixth house indicates one whose health is dependent upon his emotional state. He is susceptible to unusual diseases, especially blood disorders. He responds well to psychic healing, Reiki, and vibrational healing techniques. This is an excellent position for a psychologist or a healer. No sacrifice is too great to lessen the burdens of others for this native.

Pluto in the Seventh House

This position of Pluto indicates a strong amount of influence by the native upon his or her partners and the public. He or she may have peculiar marriage relationships. He or she may divorce because of platonic love affairs of the partner whose Pluto usually falls in the eleventh house.

Pluto in the Eighth House

A native whose Pluto is placed in the eighth house is intuitive, courageous and delves deeply into investigative work. This position indicates the native's interest in the metaphysical realms. He or she is independent and may have a tendency to be domineering. An inheritance is possible by this position of Pluto. Even though the native has good business abilities, there may be financial problems through the spouse. This native may be able to obtain knowledge of the afterlife and usually has a painless, sudden death through poisons.

Pluto in the Ninth House

Pluto placed in the ninth house indicates a native who is philosophical, religious, intuitive and enjoys travel. He or she could be or become a religious fanatic and often has strange legal entanglements.

Pluto in the Tenth House

One who has Pluto placed in his tenth house may have odd home conditions or a parent who is mentally afflicted. Notoriety may be due to the native and he may well become a dictator. Independent, a native with Pluto in his tenth house desires power, recognition and leadership. He may encounter danger through his position in life.

Pluto in the Eleventh House

This native could well be a leader of group associations. He is bohemian in nature and will sacrifice for his friends. Subject to flattery, he is social, humanitarian and devoted to a cause. His followers will either love him or hate him. If poorly aspected, he or she could be a gang leader or a criminal and lack in his moral code.

Pluto in the Twelfth House

Pluto placed in the twelfth house indicates a person who lives in seclusion and retreats from life. He is attracted to the occult, the metaphysical, and seeks the truth. If the house is ruled by a fixed sign, this native has intense emotions.

QUESTIONNAIRE

1. Is a native with his natal Sun placed in the fifth house similar to one who was born under the sign of Leo? How?

2. Describe one born with his/her Moon positioned in the first house.

3. Describe the finances of one born with his Sun in the twelfth house in his/her early years.

4. Describe the interests of a native born with his moon positioned in his sixth house.

5. Would you like a partner with his/her Mercury falling in his seventh house or a partner with his/her Mercury positioned in his/her twelfth house?

6. Do you think a native born with Venus in his/her fifth house would make a good host or hostess?

7. Describe Natal Mars falling in ones fourth house.

8. Will a native born with Jupiter in his Seventh House benefit from marriage and partnerships?

9. Would one born with Jupiter falling in his first house or on his ascendant need to watch his/her diet?

10. Describe one born with Saturn in his fifth house. Will this position of Saturn bode well for his children? Would this person prefer a younger or an older partner?

11. Does one born with Uranus falling in his seventh house have conventional ides on marriage?

Chapter 7

THE MOON'S NODES

The Moon's Nodes

The North Node, also known as the dragon's head, occurs when the Moon crosses the elliptic from south to north latitude. The North Node is known to react in a beneficial manner, similar to the planet Jupiter.

The South Node, known as the dragon's tail, is the point directly opposite the North Node. This is known to react in a negative manner, similar to the planet, Saturn.

Many astrologers, including me, use the Moon's Nodes while interpreting charts. For that reason, I am including them in this section of the book even though the nodes are neither planets nor are they asteroids.

THE MOON'S NODES IN HOUSES AND SIGNS

The North Node in the First House

The North Node in the first house, the natural house of Aries, indicates a person who is decisive, independent, inspiring, courageous, and is capable of leading others. Opportunity is offered for self-expression and honors through religious, educational and scientific endeavors.

The South Node in the First House

The South Node placed in the first house indicates one who is indecisive and dependent upon others. Loses and scandals are indicated.

It is not a good aspect for a long life. Danger to the face, eyes and head is indicated. These people need to learn to be cooperative with others.

The North Node in the Second House

North Node placed in the second house, the natural house of Taurus, indicates one who is persevering and practical, capable of developing strong partnerships or unions to benefit the community. This is a good position for learning, especially scientific subjects. It is also significant for an inheritance and accumulating possessions.

The South Node in the Second House

South Node placed in the second house indicates one who may be resentful and seeks advantage through others. It indicates financial losses, especially to the estate as well as worries about financial matters. They need to utilize their efforts and talents for a common goal and learn that people are more important than material items.

The North Node in the Third House

The North Node, placed in the third house, the natural house of Gemini, indicates one who is expressive and versatile. Favorable contacts with relatives and neighbors are indicated as well as interest in education, writing, publishing and traveling. This position indicates one who is mentally sharp.

The South Node in the Third House

The South Node, placed in the third house represents a native who is restless and tactless. He may suffer from anxiety, problems with his siblings and neighbors. Traveling is not beneficial. This native needs to consider the value of others philosophies and religions. Since the South Node is interpreted as a Saturn influence, the native whose South Node falls in the third house has a need to accomplish.

The North Node in the Fourth House

The North Node placed in the fourth house, the natural house of Cancer, indicates one who is noble, trustworthy, sympathetic and may gain through property.

The South Node in the Fourth House

The South Node placed in the fourth house may be pessimistic and self-centered. It is extremely possible that he may experience loss with land and buildings. Turmoil may exist at home and in the family.

The North Node in the Fifth House

The North Node in the Fifth House, the natural house of Leo, is favorable for popularity, children, love affairs, entertainment and sports.

The South Node in the Fifth House

The native with his South Node placed in his fifth house must be careful that he is not wasteful. It is easy for this native to be loving to others, but it is difficult for him to receive love. These people are creative and need to use their abilities for group endeavors. He or she may have problems or suffer sorrow through his children.

The North Node in the Sixth House

The North Node in the sixth house, the natural house of Virgo, is analytical, tolerant, has an interest in and is fortunate with his health, his employees, and with small animals.

The South Node in the Sixth House

The South Node positioned in the sixth house indicates poor health possibly caused by diet and a tendency to be negative. He may be taken advantage of by his employees and may suffer through the loss of small animals. He should guard against insect, animal and reptile bites. This native needs to help himself and others have a better outlook on life. This will be a challenge for him, but he will be happier for it.

The North Node in the Seventh House

The North Node in the seventh house, the natural house of Libra, indicates a native who is social and enjoys working with others. He or she is likely to have a partner who is as wise as he is wealthy.

The South Node in the Seventh House

The South Node in the seventh house indicates a rebellious and impulsive person who has problems with his or her partners. These people need to be independent; otherwise, they will be dominated.

The North Node in the Eighth House

The North Node placed in the eighth house, the natural house of Scorpio, indicates good health, a long life and an inheritance.

The South Node in the Eighth House

The South Node placed in the eighth house indicates loss of material items through deception as well as sudden death, possibly through violence.

The North Node in the Ninth House

The North Node placed in the ninth house, the natural house of Sagittarius, offers success in the areas of law, religion and journeys to foreign countries. The native may have prophetic dreams.

The South Node in the Ninth House

The South Node placed in the native's ninth house indicates trouble while traveling, especially to foreign countries and the possibility of imprisonment. There is a lack of faith and the native may experience strange dreams. They need to cultivate and learn from people in their environment and stop moving from place to place.

The North Node in the Tenth House

The North Node placed in the tenth house, the natural house of Capricorn, brings honors, recognition and awards in connection to achievements in the natives career.

The South Node in the Tenth House

The South Node in the tenth house is often an egotist, but if he achieves the acclaim he yearns for, he will not be able to handle the pressure fame will bring.

The North Node in the Eleventh House

The North Node in the eleventh house, the natural house of Aquarius, indicates that good friends and group associations will help this native achieve his dreams.

The South Node in the Eleventh House

The South Node placed in the eleventh house indicates the native makes unwise friendships and associations. He suffers many disappointments through his hopes and wishes.

The North Node in the Twelfth House

The North Node placed in the twelfth house, the natural house of Pisces, indicates success through seclusion, metaphysical endeavors and institutions.

The South Node in the Twelfth House

The South Node placed in the twelfth house indicates a possibility of imprisonment or of being institutionalized. This is a poor placement for the native's health.

NOTES:

When a solar or lunar eclipse occurs at the exact degree of the South Node, a death or extreme change is likely to occur in the coming year.

QUESTIONNAIRE

1. When does the North node or dragon's head occur?

2. How does the north node react?

3. What does the dragon's tail or south node occur?

4. How does it react?

5. Are the nodes considered planets or asteroids?

Chapter 8

PART OF FORTUNE

The Part of Fortune is the most commonly used of the Arabic parts. It is a point equally distant from the ascendant as the Moon is to the Sun in longitude. It is said to benefit the house that it is located in.

First House

If the Part of Fortune falls into the first house, the native benefits from his own work or industry.

Second House

If the Part of Fortune falls in the natives second house he or she is apt to gain through property and employment. Friendships through business will be advantageous for him.

Third House

If the native's Part of Fortune falls into his third house, his travels will be profitable; he may succeed through intellectual endeavors and through relatives.

Fourth House

If the native's Part of Fortune falls into his fourth house, he will gain through property or hidden things such as minerals or metals. If it is verified by other aspects, he may gain through legacy.

Fifth House

If the Part of Fortune falls into the fifth house, the native will gain through investments and children, unless it is poorly aspected. If it is, the native will need to develop his creativity rather than dwell on love affairs, gambling, speculation or children. He also needs to become more motivated and develop qualities of optimism and enthusiasm.

Sixth House

The Part of Fortune falling in the sixth house indicates that aunts, uncles, small pets, servants and employment in the service of others will be of benefit to him.

Seventh House

The Part of Fortune falling into the seventh house indicates that the native will succeed through others and in partnership. If this position is afflicted, then the contrary will be true.

Eighth House

The Part of Fortune falling into the eighth house indicates that the native will gain by a legacy of through others money.

Ninth House

The Part of Fortune falling in the ninth house indicates long trips, gain through educational institutions, foreigners, inventions or literature.

Tenth House

The Part of Fortune falling in the tenth house indicates that the native may benefit through favorable circumstances and events that assist him to rise in his career. He may receive honors.

Eleventh House

The Part of Fortune falling into the eleventh house indicates that the native gains through his friends. It also benefits him in achieving his hopes and wishes.

Twelfth House

The Part of Fortune falling into the native's twelfth house indicates that he will benefit as a truth seeker rather than retreating from society. As he ages, he will attract possessions.

QUESTIONNAIRE

1. What is the Part of Fortune?

Chapter 9

THE ASCENDING SIGNS

The ascending sign is the rising sign or the cusp of the first house. It represents the way the world sees you even though you may feel differently at heart. It is the manner in which you project yourself to the public. This is determined by the degree of the zodiac on the eastern horizon at the specific time and location you were born. Each sign takes approximately two hours to rise over the horizon.

Quite often, an astrologer is asked to guess what Sun Sign a native was born under. It is common for one to guess the rising sign or the planet's ruler closest to the rising sign. For instance, if your ascending sign is Pisces but Jupiter is conjunct or within a few degrees of the ascendant one might think you are a Sagittarius ascendant. (Jupiter rules Sagittarius.) If you are a Taurus Sun, but have an Aries ascendant, one might believe you are an Aries Sun Sign because that is the manner in which you project yourself to the world.

Aries Rising

Aries rising, ruled by the planet Mars, is enthusiastic, courageous and impulsive. Independent and self-reliant, he is a self starter. He has a quick wit, a friendly manner and is honest and to the point. Don't let him or her fool you though. All is not as it may seem. Oftentimes, Aries ascendants have an unhappy childhood and under that wide smile and outgoing manner is a quick temper.

Physically, he is often short in stature with a muscular body and strong arms. He may suffer from headaches, earaches, sinus problems and upper teeth problems. He is active, walks quickly and dances well. Fond of his freedom, he will search for an independent partner.

Taurus Rising

Taurus ascending, ruled by Venus, is friendly, has a beautiful smile and a gentle manner. Patient, she is reserved, good humored, honorable and trustworthy. Don't push this native. She is stubborn and difficult to change once she makes up her mind. Fond of beauty, the arts and nature, she is loyal and happiest when in a stable relationship. He or she is usually found working in a creative field, the entertainment business, banking or a building trade.

Physically, Taurus rising has soft, come-hither round eyes. He or she winks often; accompanied by a smile. When making a decision, they often sigh as though they are completely worn out. They enjoy the scent of oven-baked bread, freshly mown lawns or hay. They will never forget the scent of a special perfume or an aftershave lotion. Their skin is easily irritated and they often have naturally curly hair. A lock may fall directly in the center of his or her forehead conveying, "When she was good, she was very, very good, but when she was bad she was very, very bad."

Gemini Rising

Gemini rising, ruled by Mercury, is friendly, confident and cheerful. Their mind is quick and they have a lively sense of humor. Physically, Gemini ascendants features are sharp. The women wear their hair short and mostly in awry for there is no time in her life for styling sessions. He or she is attracted to other air and fire signs.

Cancer Rising

Cancer rising is changeable, curious, and moody. His eyes are hypnotic and melancholy. Happiest near water, he loves all things nautical. Although he is an excellent wood carver, printmaker and craftsman, he also enjoys buying and selling. Attracted to Taurus, Pisces, Scorpio, and Virgo, he will choose the one who offers him the security and unconditional love he needs.

As for the physical description, this rising sign's eyes are always moving; their eyelids are prominent and he or she often smiles with his or her mouth closed. They speak softly at one moment and aggressively at another, changing with their many moods. Their laughter crashes and tumbles, like waves rolling onto shore. All of their extra weight is stored in a stomach pouch. His or her dropping shoulders may slouch. Cancer ascendants often walk with a sideways step as though they are sliding along a shoreline. This person prefers casual clothes that allow him freedom of movement.

Leo Rising

This rising sign, ruled by the Sun, is proud, compelling and enjoys being the center of attention. Leo rising is strong-willed and capable of taking charge. He lives and loves to the limit, expecting to be waited on and treated well. He or she is often found among entertainers and sports figures. When he or she looks for a mate, he or she will gravitate to the air and fire signs of Gemini, Aries, Leo, Libra, and Sagittarius and to his opposite sign, Aquarius.

Physically, Leo rising's trademark is his thick, lustrous hair. They have soft, large, round or almond shaped eyes that have a playful sparkle to them. His or her smiles are beautiful. Their noses are either long and straight, or small. Men nearly always have facial hair, mustaches, beards, etc. Both the female and male ascendants primp and preen in public. You won't find this ascendant slouching for Leo rising has excellent posture.

Virgo Rising

Virgo rising, ruled by Mercury, enjoys bringing order out of chaos. Tidying up, sorting and performing services for others please them. They are often found in the fields of medicine, natural health, teaching or in the service fields. In regard to health, they often have sinus problems.

Physically, Virgo rising seldom smiles with his mouth open. When he or she does, you may notice the crowded teeth and small mouth as far as width is concerned. His or her hair is usually shining and clean. Careful with their actions and speech, they desire to keep their reputations spotless.

Libra Rising

Libra rising, ruled by Venus, is ambitious yet hesitant to make a decision. Weighing the scales back and forth indefinitely, one might arrive at the conclusion that she is indecisive. A social creature, she loves beauty and enjoys musical and artistic pursuits She is gracious, diplomatic, and charming.

Physically, Libra rising has soft, wide open eyes. Their lips are often bow shaped and one will most always find a Libra chattering. They walk softly, but firmly. When entertaining, they display their finest linens, china, and silver. As far as their diet is concerned, they prefer an assortment and often skip meals filling in with sweets. In regard to sports, you may find Libra rising on the golf or tennis courts.

Scorpio Rising

Scorpio rising, ruled by Pluto, is intense, cautious and will carry a project through to the end. Clever and mysterious, Scorpio rising has the ability to reconstruct his life when it collapses. Proud, with high standards, he or she never forgets an insult or a kindness. This rising sign is an excellent historian and linguist.

Physically, Scorpio ascending is poker faced when concealing his emotions. He is short and walks with grace.

Sagittarius Rising

Sagittarius rising, ruled by Jupiter, is energetic, friendly with an open nature and a carefree smile. Cheerful and outgoing, he or she is resourceful with a sense of humor and a love of sports. An excellent communicator, Sagittarius rising prefers to come and go as he or she pleases.

Physically, Sagittarius rising has warm, friendly eyes and speaks with his mouth wide open. He grins a lot, squinting as he does so. When speaking, Sagittarius rising blurts out words or phrases whether anyone else is speaking or not. When explaining himself, he interrupts his phrases or words laughing. Proud of his education, he may use many quotes of famous people. He or she prefers casual or sports attire-a lot of denim and sports jackets. "Don't fence me in" is a phrase he shares with Aquarius and Aries for he loves his freedom.

Capricorn Rising

Capricorn rising, ruled by Saturn, is shy and timid as a child. As an adult, he or she is calm, quiet and modest. Independent, he is shrewd, financially adept, and would prefer to be self-employed. A good listener and a hard worker, Capricorn rising has a dry sense of humor. Capricorn rising, like the sun sign, needs to accomplish. He will do most anything to stay busy.

Physically, Capricorn ascending often has high cheekbones, large eyes and a smile that turns down slightly at the corners. He is short to medium in stature. Afflicted with rheumatism of his or her knees, this rising sign is prone to asthma and bronchitis.

Aquarius Rising

Aquarius rising, ruled by the planet Uranus, is intelligent, tolerant, dogmatic, far seeing and freedom loving. Humanitarians, they are involved with everyone and concerned with socially balanced values. They do not dress for fashion but usually wear casual clothing. He or she is the best friend one could ask for.

Physically, Aquarius rising is tall, slender with sparkling eyes and a genuine smile. He or she has a prominent nose, highly arched brows, and wears his hair in disarray.

Pisces Rising

Pisces rising, ruled by Neptune, is a sensitive, kind and considerate dreamer that oftentimes has problems dealing with reality. Clairvoyant and psychic, he or she is a natural healer. Gentle and spiritual, Pisces ascendants often work in prisons, institutions, nursing homes and orphanages. They enjoy living near water and long to make the world a more beautiful and gentler place.

Physically, when a Pisces rising is deep in thought or conversation, his head will tilt from side to side. He will wrinkle his forehead and glance at the floor when he is considering something. A Pisces ascendant does not want to rock the boat. They would rather retreat to another section of the room than enter into an argument. They walk softly, gliding along gracefully and are fine dancers, taking care not to step on their partner's feet. Pisces women enjoy wearing flowing dresses while the Pisces male ascendant wears well-fitting sports clothes. If they are not feeling well or are down, they would just as soon appear in rags and total disarray.

Questionnaire

1. What is the Ascendent or rising sign?

2. How is it determined?

3. Describe Taurus rising.

4. Describe Leo rising.

5. Does Scorpio rising easily forgive an injury?

6. Does Virgo rising often smile with his mouth open?

Chapter 10

THE ASPECTS

The planets are considered to be in aspect when they are specific degrees or angles to each other.

Astrologers usually use both major and minor aspects, allowing six degrees upon approach and two degrees upon departure with the exception of the Sun and Moon, commonly referred to as the lights. Most astrologers, including me, allow ten degrees upon the approach of a planet aspecting the lights (Sun and Moon); five degrees departing. An aspect is at its strongest when *conjunct* the natal planet or in a stationary position.

Following, are the most important aspects to be taken into consideration:

The Conjunction 0-6 degrees Power and energy are offered. This aspect may be considered positive or negative depending upon the planets involved. The same is true when using astrology in weather predictions.

The Sextile 60 degrees This aspect offers the opportunity to be productive and creative. It is considered to be favorable and likely to produce fair weather.

The Square 90 degrees This aspect brings obstacles and stress.

Change may be required. As far as weather is concerned, both the square and opposition produce storms.

The Trine 120 degrees This aspect is harmonious, creative and easy. It is said to be a favorable aspect and is likely to produce fair weather.

Quincunx 150 degrees This is an inharmonious aspect. said to be malefic or unfavorable. Adjustment is required.

Opposition 180 degrees This aspect is inharmonious and calls for cooperation. Conflicts are brought about by others that may cause change. In regard to weather conditions, this aspect produces storms.

Parallel 1 degree The parallel aspect offers power.

Other Aspects

Grand Cross Challenges.
Cardinal Cross It is required that the native motivate himself.
Fixed Cross Requires an emotional creative outlet.
Mutable Cross The native is required to be adaptable to changes in the environment but remain decisive.

T-Square
There is imbalance. The sign of the missing leg must be developed.

The Yod
The yod is the point at which one sextile conjuncts two in-conjuncts, appearing much like an elongated triangle. The area where the in-conjuncts join creates a feeling that you have been placed here to do something out of the ordinary. This point is referred to as the Finger of God, the Finger of Fate.

Critical Degrees

When you are interpreting a chart, you will also want to take into consideration critical degrees existing in the natal chart. A planet's strength in the horoscope is said to be stronger when it is within three degrees of a critical degree. Consider this when interpreting a horary chart as well.

The critical degrees of the Cardinal Signs (Aries, Libra, Cancer and Capricorn) are:

1 degree
13 degrees
26 degrees

The critical degrees of the Mutable Signs (Gemini, Sagittarius, Virgo and Pisces) are:

4 degrees
17 degrees

The critical degrees of the Fixed Signs (Taurus, Scorpio, Leo and Aquarius) are:

9 degrees
15 degrees
21 degrees

ASPECTS TO THE SUN

Moon/Sun

+The Moon in favorable aspect to the Sun indicates that the native is in harmony with his parents, partners and the public. This is a positive aspect for romance and friendship.

-If the Moon forms an unfavorable aspect to the Sun, the native may be feeling poorly, discontented, and out of sorts with his parents, partners and the public.

Mercury/Sun

+Mercury in favorable aspect to the Sun indicates that the native is clear thinking, prudent and practical. In transit, this aspect indicates that it is a good time to reorganize. It is an excellent aspect for success in business matters and travel.

-Mercury in unfavorable aspect to the Sun indicates the native may be inclined to over-work and become nervous. He may also be absentminded and lack focus, and clarity.

Venus/Sun

+Venus in favorable aspect to the Sun indicates the powers of attraction, love, social life, and enjoyment of beauty, art, music and nature. It also indicates that the native is generous, warmhearted, and affectionate. This is a good aspect for making money and for romance.

-Venus in unfavorable aspect to the Sun indicates poor health caused by overindulgence, eating and drinking too much. It also indicates extravagance and problems with love.

Mars/Sun

+Mars in good aspect to the Sun is energetic, determined, vital, courageous and confident. He is frank, ambitious, commanding, and generous with the power to lead. This aspect is excellent for sports activities.

-Mars in poor aspect to the Sun increases the tendency toward accidents and fevers. If one has heart problems, this is not a good period to overdo. The native may be rash, outspoken, in poor temper, aggressive defensive, destructive and headstrong. Loss of esteem, cuts, burns, bruises could result. It is also an aspect indicating surgical operations. Because the lights (Sun and Moon) represent the eyes, there may also be a problem with one or both of the eyes.

+Jupiter/Sun

Jupiter in good aspect to the Sun denotes good health, expansion, a farseeing attitude, success and good judgment. It indicates one who is sympathetic, honest, generous, sincere, and honest. He or she is fond of sports and could gain in speculation. Friends who are influential or well-off may benefit the native. For a woman, it may indicate a favorable time for love and marriage.

-Jupiter/Sun

Jupiter in unfavorable aspect to the Sun indicates poor health during the latter part of life as well as financial loss through speculation, investments, gambling and legal affairs. One might be egotistical and extravagant with this aspect.

+Saturn/Sun

Saturn in good aspect to the Sun is serious, practical with good organizational talents. He will rise in life and succeed through his own efforts and qualities which are considerable.

-Saturn/Sun

This aspect denotes a weak constitution and poor health. It is an unfavorable time for promoting business affairs. Obstacles, delays, and sorrow cause losses. His ambitions are never realized due to opposition and jealousy.

+Neptune/Sun

This aspect offers a philosophical, inspirational, spiritual, or religious outlook on life. The native is often interested in photography, metaphysical, and psychic research. The emotions are refined; the native is sympathetic and generous. He enjoys boating, traveling, art, nature and beauty.

-Neptune/Sun

Neptune in poor aspect to the Sun indicates fraud, strange love affairs, problems through children, speculation, gambling and alcohol. The native may be mediumistic and experience out-of-the-ordinary dreams. He needs to watch his health for he could suffer from an illness that may be difficult to diagnose. Conjunctions may be positive or negative; however, if Neptune is conjunct with the Sun, the native will, more than likely, have problems keeping his partners.

+Pluto/Sun

This aspect indicates that the native has a powerful influence over others. He will discard anything that stands in the way of achieving his goal. This person has leadership qualities.

-This aspect indicates that the native overestimates himself and is arrogant.

North Node/Sun

+This is a significant aspect of favorable contact with males. It is a favorable aspect for working together and for public relations.

-The negative aspect of the North Node to the Sun may signify the termination of a relationship or at least of an unpleasant atmosphere in either working as a team or living together.

MC/Sun

+The favorable aspect of the Sun to the Midheaven signifies a positive attitude or success in career matters.

-The unfavorable aspects of the Sun to the Midheaven or MC indicate a lack of clarity in one's goals.

Sun/Ascendant

+The favorable aspects of the Sun to the ascendant indicate meetings with males and advantageous meetings with the public.

-The unfavorable aspects of Sun to the ascendant indicate misplaced confidence in males or in the public.

ASPECTS TO THE MOON

Moon/Mercury

+ In its positive aspect, Moon/Mercury indicates that the native is kind, thoughtful, discreet, adaptable and has an active intellect and good reasoning powers. In transit, it may indicate a short trip and conversations with women or the mother.

-Moon/Mercury negative aspects indicate that the native enjoys gossip, may lie and has changing views and sensitive nerves.

Moon/Venus

+In its positive aspect Moon/Venus indicates that the native is artistic, affectionate and warm hearted. In transit, it indicates a happy family life or romance. It may also indicate a marriage gifted with many offspring.

-In its negative aspect, Moon/Venus indicates that the native is moody, shy and easily led. In transit, it indicates moodiness, irritability and problems in ones love life.

Moon/Mars

+This aspect indicates the native is open, honest, sincere and has a strong will. In transit, it may bring a love union or a relationship.

-In its negative aspects, Moon/Mars indicate that the native is irritable, impulsive and excitable. He will oftentimes rebel against any restriction. In transit, this aspect may indicate the native may become argumentative, is irritable and intolerant for the duration of this aspect. He or she may have problems with his or her stomach or thyroid gland during this time.

Moon/Jupiter

+The positive aspect indicates that the native is kind, religious or spiritual, helpful, generous and popular in the public eye. In transit, it may indicate a marriage, social success and successful contacts with a foreign country or foreigners.

-The negative aspect indicates unpopularity, opposition and an indifferent attitude. In transit, it may indicate problems in marriage, legal conflicts and squandering ones assets.

Moon/Saturn

+This aspect indicates that the native is thoughtful, attentive, considerate and conscientious. He is self-controlled, serious and often alone. This native may build his career upon family tradition.

-The negative aspect of Moon/Saturn indicates concerns due to the family or wife, separation from the mother or wife and isolation. It may indicate a lonely woman.

Moon/Uranus

+Moon/Uranus indicates that the native is emotionally excitable, ambitious, self-willed and is interested in metaphysical subjects.

-Moon/Uranus indicates that the native is self-willed and stubborn. More than likely, he suffers from anxiety and overstrains his nerves.

Moon/Neptune

+Moon/Neptune in its positive aspects indicates that the native is sensitive, imaginative, perceptive and inspirational. More than likely he has intense dreams, perhaps even precognitive dreams. It is easy for this person to relax.

-Moon/Neptune negative aspects indicate that the native may be subject of being exploited by others. He or she may be lazy or have unstable emotions.

Note: If there is a -Moon/Neptune aspect with Saturn in a negative aspect, the native may have sists.

Moon/Pluto

+Moon/Pluto in its positive aspect indicates that the native may experience a deep expression of feeling, and will pursue his goals fanatically without regard for others. He or she is capable of transforming images into reality.

-Moon/Pluto negative indicates emotional disturbances, shocks, and violent outbursts.

Moon/North Node

+Moon/North Node in its positive aspect indicates associations with females.

-Moon/North Node in a negative aspect indicates separations from women, the mother, or the family.

Moon/Ascendant

+In its positive aspect, this indicates pleasant contacts with women or the mother.

-In its negative aspect, Moon/Ascendant indicates a disharmonious relationship with women, the mother or the wife.

Moon/Midheaven

+Moon/Midheaven in its positive aspect indicates the native has deep feelings and spiritual values. He enjoys taking care of others and has an appreciation for his home and family.

-Moon/Midheaven in its negative aspect indicates many changes in the native's life.

ASPECTS TO MERCURY

Venus/Mercury

+The positive aspects of Venus to Mercury indicate a quick wit, romantic thoughts, a poet or a romance writer. The native has an appreciation of beauty, art and has a cheerful attitude.

-Venus/Mercury

The negative aspects of Venus to Mercury indicate one who may be conceited, hypersensitive, and squander his or her money.

+Mars/Mercury

A positive Mars/Mercury aspect indicates one who has an active mind, sharp wit and travels. He may join in debates or be a critic.

-Mars/Mercury

This aspect indicates one who is argumentative, obstinate, and is nervous. If this is an aspect in transit, the person may have problems with transportation or suffer from fevers.

+Jupiter/Mercury

This aspect indicates one who has good intellect, is optimistic, and is a successful businessman, speaker or writer. If this is an aspect in transit, it is a favorable time for decisions or signing contracts.

-Jupiter/Mercury

The negative aspect of Jupiter to Mercury indicates arrogance, absentmindedness, fraud, and lack of tact.

Saturn/Mercury

+ The positive aspects of Saturn to Mercury indicate one who is capable of good organization, is logical and concentrates well. He is industrious and philosophical.

-Saturn/Mercury

The negative aspects of Saturn to Mercury indicates one who is reserved, shy and may either be slow or depressed. This native may have had a difficult childhood. Separations are indicated. If this is an aspect in transit, it is not advisable to take a trip for pleasure at this time. This aspect could also indicate speech or hearing problems.

Uranus/Mercury

+ The positive aspects of Uranus in aspect to Mercury indicate an interest in mathematics, physics, astrology, science, or engineering. This native is inventive, innovative, and intellectual.

-The negative aspects of Uranus in aspect to Mercury indicate a native who is nervous, scattered and has too many things going at one time. He has a problem focusing on his goals, overestimates himself and may have contradicting viewpoints.

Neptune/Mercury

+The favorable aspects of Neptune to Mercury indicate one who is psychic, spiritual, imaginative, compassionate, and intuitive. He may be capable of automatic writing, have the ability to be an inspirational speaker, an actor or an actress. If this is an aspect in transit, it may indicate a voyage over water.

-The unfavorable aspects of Neptune to Mercury indicate a confused state of mind, fraud, deception, and absentmindedness. There may be a psychic or nerve disorder. In any case, he or she should refrain from taking alcohol and drugs. If this is an aspect in transit, delay signing papers and making important decisions until the aspect passes.

Pluto/Mercury

+The favorable aspects of Pluto/Mercury indicate a successful speaker, orator, or writer; one who is capable of influencing the public. This aspect strengthens the native's mentality and indicates that the native may have memories of past lives.

-The unfavorable aspects of Pluto/Mercury indicate pre-mature action, irritability and one who is stubborn. This native may be capable of fraudulent misrepresentation.

Node/Mercury

+The node in favorable aspect to Mercury indicates contact with neighbors and relatives.

- The node in unfavorable aspect to Mercury indicates inharmonious contacts with associations.

MC/Mercury

+This is a good aspect for setting ones goals.

-Mercury in poor aspect to the Midheaven is an indication of scattered energies. Delay making plans or setting goals at this time.

Mercury/Ascendant

+Mercury in favorable aspect to the ascendant indicates discussions, meetings, visits to the home, receiving letters, faxes and e-mails.

-Mercury in unfavorable aspect to the ascendant indicates an unfriendly attitude. The native may judge others unfairly or perhaps, he is being judged unfairly.

ASPECTS TO VENUS

Venus/Mars

+The harmonious aspects of Venus/Mars indicate love, passion, desire, creativity, increased confidence, and generosity.

-The inharmonious aspects of Venus/Mars indicate problems in love and marriage as well as danger of loss.

Venus/Jupiter

+The harmonious aspects of Jupiter to Venus indicate that the native is refined, sympathetic, thoughtful, popular, good humored, optimistic and is capable handling substantial wealth. As a transit, this is an excellent aspect for love, becoming engaged, and marriage. It is also a good aspect for purchasing jewelry and objects of art.

-The inharmonious aspects of Jupiter to Venus indicate that the native may desire wealth, jewels, and other luxuries, but must make do with what he has. This is not a good aspect for saving money, nor is it a good aspect for love and marriage. He or she is too fond of luxuries and pleasures. This may result in loss and perhaps, illness if the native imbibes too much.

Venus/Saturn

+The harmonious aspects of Venus/Saturn indicate that the native is reserved, loyal and faithful. He or she may be attracted to a partner who is much younger or older than themselves.

-The inharmonious aspects of Venus/Saturn indicate loneliness, duty, problems in love, jealousy, and separations. As far as transiting aspects are concerned, one will feel unloved, ugly, and out of sorts with this transit.

Venus/Uranus

+The harmonious aspects between Venus and Uranus indicate artistic and musical abilities as well as a sudden improvement in the native's love life.

-The inharmonious aspects between Venus and Uranus indicate one who is moody, nervous, sensitive and unfaithful.

Venus/Neptune

+The positive aspects of Venus/Neptune indicate one who is talented in music, art and is a romantic at heart. He or she enjoys beauty, has high ideals and may be interested in the metaphysical.

-The negative aspects of Venus/Neptune indicates jealousy, crudeness, a lack of tact and the end of an illusion.

Venus/Pluto

+The positive aspects of Venus/Pluto indicate a loyal friend and one who has a warm personality with an empathetic nature. As a transiting aspect, it indicates a powerful attraction combined with a heightened sexual drive. He or she has an appreciation of art and universal love.

-The negative aspects of Venus/Pluto indicate a jealous and possessive nature. The native is insecure and feels unloved. As a transit, relationships may become inharmonious. The native may elope or marry without ceremony.

Venus/Node

+ The positive aspects of Venus to the Node indicate the native is adaptable and good hearted with many female contacts. In transit, this aspect may bring a romantic or artistic contact.

-The negative aspects of Venus to the Node indicate a disagreeable nature and a lack of harmony, especially with female friends and relations.

Venus/MC

+The native who has a positive aspect between Venus and the Midheaven is adaptable, with associations or friends who are artists or designers.

-The disharmonious aspect between Venus and the Midheaven is likely to be difficult to get along with.

Venus/Ascendant

+Venus in positive aspect to his or her ascendant indicates a pleasing environment, visits with women, including sisters. In transit, this is a favorable time for purchasing clothing and improving your environment. It may also signify a love affair.

-Venus in an unfavorable aspect to the ascendant indicates one squanders his or her money and lacks taste.

ASPECTS TO MARS

Mars/Jupiter

+The favorable aspects of Mars/Jupiter indicate a native who is generous, honorable, ambitious, capable of leadership, a successful career and success with negotiations. This placement may offer the possibility of an inheritance if it is validated elsewhere in the natal chart. This transit indicates one who has managerial abilities and will help others to help themselves. In transit, this aspect is favorable for signing contracts, entering into negotiations, becoming engaged or marrying. It is also a favorable aspect for births. When Mars is conjunct Jupiter in transit, there is more than a good chance that the earth's climatic conditions are favorable for rain or snow.

-Mars in unfavorable aspect to Jupiter indicates that the native rebels against the laws of society, against parents and superiors. Conflicts will arise in marriage. In transit, a negative Mars/Jupiter aspect may result in an arrest, an unfavorable legal decision or a traffic ticket.

Mars/Saturn

+Mars/Saturn in favorable aspect indicates that the native is self-reliant, confident, courageous and determined. He has the endurance and energy to overcome difficulties that may confront him. This native may be reckless.

-Mars/Saturn in a negative aspect may indicate a native who is harsh, self-willed, and obstinate. In transit, this may indicate an accident, resulting in a broken bone or an inflammation of the bone or tendon. It may also result in an illness, suffocation, or a a period of separation. If the native is not forthright and honest, he or she may be apprehended.

Mars/Uranus

+Mars/Uranus in its positive aspect indicates a freedom-loving individual who is determined, courageous and unusual. This native is self-confident, energetic, impulsive, ambitious, and intellectual. He may be an inventor, an engineer or be employed by the government. He is most likely interested in metaphysics, astrology and psychology.

-Mars/Uranus in its negative aspect indicates a native who is restless, erratic, irritable, eccentric, and excitable. There is danger through firearms, explosions, lightning, fire, machinery, and transportation. Accidents are probable as well as sudden unpleasant events.

Mars/Neptune

+A positive Mars/Neptune aspect indicates a love for travel, especially over the water, interest in the metaphysical, and psychic. The native is generous, enthusiastic, romantic, and adventurous. This person enjoys water sports.

-Mars/Neptune in its negative aspect may indicate accidents through water or fire or loss through scandal, fraud and deceit. There is danger through alcohol, poisons, drugs, and fire. Psychically, it may indicate hallucinations. In transit, there is danger through all of the above. One who is born with this aspect should not drink alcohol or take drugs. This native may have allergies and should also be careful of prescriptive drugs.

Mars/Pluto

+One born with a positive Mars/Pluto aspect is likely to possess an enormous amount of courage, energy, self-confidence and ambition. He or she may be a leader of world reforms.

-Mars/Pluto in its negative aspect indicates a native who is ruthless in pursuit of his goals. He may be brutal or suffer from assaults and injuries. This person may be violent, foolhardy and restless. He must learn to analyze his purpose for taking action. This aspect also indicates one who may enjoy taking drugs.

Mars/North Node

+The positive aspect of Mars/North Node indicates good teamwork and partnership. It may also indicate harmonious physical relationships.

-The negative aspect of Mars/North Node indicates arguments and possibly separation of partners or associations.

Mars/Ascendant

+This native is capable of leading others and of achieving his goals.

-Mars/Ascendant in its negative position indicates one who is aggressive, argumentative and enjoys fighting. In transit, Mars/Ascendant in a negative position or conjunction may indicate an accident or a surgical operation. If other aspects point to it, this aspect may indicate an assault.

Mars/Midheaven

+Mars in positive aspect to the midheaven indicates a native who is independent, prudent and capable of making decisions. He is capable of succeeding in his goals and career. This is a positive aspect for changing careers or fulfilling goals.

-Mars/Midheaven in a negative aspect indicates that the native is impulsive, lacks direction in his goals and involves himself in disputes. This is an aspect one might be fired under if other aspects in the chart validate it.

ASPECTS TO JUPITER

Saturn/Jupiter

+This aspect indicates that the native will diligently and patiently work alone in order to accomplish one's goals. The native is intelligent, serious, philosophical and honest.

-The negative aspects of Saturn/Jupiter indicate poor judgment, especially in speculative ventures as well as losses through litigation, banks, property, and land. This aspect also signifies that the native may have problems through his own misrepresentation and lack of honesty.

Uranus/Jupiter

+This native has unexpected windfalls throughout his life and the possibility of receiving an inheritance. He or she is optimistic, intuitive and has the good fortune to be in the right place at the right time. Philosophical, he is adventurous and perceptive.

-The negative aspects of Uranus/Jupiter indicate that the native is freedom loving, obstinate, tactless and argumentative. Unfortunately, the native misses good opportunities.

Neptune/Jupiter

+This native is musical, artistic, spiritual, and generous. Interested in metaphysical subjects, he or she is compassionate. The native may speculate and receive windfalls without effort.

-The negative aspects of Neptune/Jupiter indicate a financial loss through speculation and squandering.

Pluto/Jupiter

+This aspect indicates that the native is optimistic, positive and generous. He is able to focus upon the root of a matter, get down to basics and avoid the superficial. He can also lighten a stressful or serious matter. More than likely, he or she has the capability to be a powerful leader and may achieve fame and recognition.

-This person is likely to have conflicts with authorities, especially in legal matters. He or she tends to be forceful and overbearing with impossible goals and relies on others. His attitude is destructive. He should not speculate for in financial matters, there is the possibility of losing everything.

Node/Jupiter

The positive aspects of Node/Jupiter indicate that the native works well with others. He or she is tactful and will have beneficial contacts. In transit, Node/Jupiter in favorable aspect may bring a beneficial partner into one's life.

-The negative aspect of Node/Jupiter indicates one who looks out for himself and is anti-social.

Jupiter/Ascendant

+The native is generous, successful, and has a pleasant and positive attitude with his associations. Beneficial contacts and a well-furnished home are indicated. Since Jupiter represents expansion; the native may gain weight during this transit.

-The negative aspects indicate one who rebels, squanders his assets, and has a negative attitude toward others.

Jupiter/Midheaven

+This aspect indicates a native who is happy and optimistic. He or she has the ability to focus upon his or her goals and succeed.

-This aspect indicates a change in career and circumstances.

ASPECTS TO SATURN

Uranus/Saturn

+Uranus/Saturn in a positive aspect indicates that the native is intuitive, perceptive and determined. This individual may persevere and endure difficult or dangerous situations.

-Uranus/Saturn in its negative aspect may bring about arguments, separations and emotional upsets that may result in violence. Changes in destiny may be due to unforeseen events resulting in a lack or loss of the native's freedom.

Neptune/Saturn

+In its positive aspect, the native is intuitive, cautious and has the ability to focus or concentrate. He is interested in the mystical and psychic. The native has the possibility of succeeding in a job or career connected with the sea or liquids such as oil. He may also be fortunate through the elderly, property, and inheritances.

-Saturn/Neptune in its negative aspect indicates a loss through fraud, scandal or deception. If the native has a poor diet, he or she is likely to become ill and hospitalized. Strange accidents may occur, requiring hospitalization.

Pluto/Saturn

+Pluto/Saturn in its favorable aspects indicates that the native is serious, reliable and has great endurance and willpower. He is able to overcome the most difficult challenges and complete difficult assignments.

-Pluto/Saturn in its negative aspects indicates a native who is an egotist in pursuit of his own goals. He or she may be jealous, dishonest, and cruel. In transit, it may mean the loss of everything.

Node/Saturn

+Node/Saturn in its positive aspects indicates one who has beneficial associations or contacts who are older.

-Node/Saturn in its negative aspects indicates a problem of cooperation with one's partners or associations. The native may be shy and inhibited.

Saturn/Ascendant

+Saturn/Ascendant in its positive aspect may represent one who prefers being with those older than he. This aspect may bring a loss of weight.

-Saturn/Ascendant in its negative aspect may indicate the native is depressed, lonely and living in poverty or a poor environment. Transiting Saturn conjunct the ascendant indicates that the native may require dental treatment.

Saturn/Midheaven

+Saturn/Midheaven in its positive aspects indicates that the native is constant in his goals in life.

-Saturn/Midheaven in its negative aspects indicate one who abandons his goals due to depression or inhibitions.

ASPECTS TO URANUS

Neptune/Uranus

+Neptune/Uranus in its favorable aspect indicates that the native is intuitive, inspirational and attracted to all things in the psychic and metaphysical realms.

-Neptune/Uranus in its negative aspects indicates instability, a lack of vitality, and psychic confusion.

Pluto/Uranus

+Pluto/Uranus in its positive aspects indicates that the native is restless, creative, active and interested in metaphysics. As a transit, this aspect may signify a move or a re-organization of living conditions.

-Pluto/Uranus in its negative aspects indicates one who loses focus, scatters his energies, is impatient and may be violent, depending upon other aspects. As a transit, it may bring violence, clashes with authorities, or an accident.

Uranus/North Node

+Uranus/North Node in its positive aspects indicates that the native may have brief relationships and eccentric, or unusual friends.

-Uranus/North Node in its negative aspects indicates that the native is restless when he or she is with others.

Uranus/Ascendant

+Uranus/Ascendant in its positive aspect indicates that the native enjoys change. He or she may be employed in the field of technology.

-Uranus/Ascendant in its negative aspects indicates a native who is restless and irritable, causing upsets to those who live and work with him. As a transit, it may indicate an accident.

Uranus/Midheaven

+Uranus/Midheaven in its positive aspect indicates that the native is prudent, visionary and will pursue out-of-the-ordinary goals or a career successfully. As a transit, this may indicate a change of career or advancement in his field.

-Uranus/Midheaven in its negative aspects indicates a native who is excitable, has a bad temper and is unreliable. He or she may change careers often.

ASPECTS TO NEPTUNE

Pluto/Neptune

+Pluto/Neptune in its favorable aspects indicates a native who is sensitive, imaginative and has an interest in the mystical areas of life.

-Pluto/Neptune in its unfavorable aspects indicates one who is obsessive and confused. He or she may be addicted to alcohol, drugs or nicotine. In transit, it may bring a loss accompanied with much sorrow.

North Node/Neptune

+North Node/Neptune in its positive aspects indicates that the native may be unrealistic in his expectations of relatives and associations.

-North Node/Neptune in its negative aspects indicates that the native may be anti-social and deceive his or her associations.

Ascendant/Neptune

+Ascendant/Neptune in its positive aspects indicates that the native is impressionable and compassionate.

-Ascendant/Neptune indicates that the native may become disillusioned or deceived.

Midheaven/Neptune

+Midheaven/Neptune in its positive aspect bestows an interest in investigating the paranormal and supernatural.

-Midheaven/Neptune in negative aspect indicates that the native may feel insecure in pursuing his goals. There is a strong chance he is likely to be deceived.

ASPECTS OF PLUTO

Pluto/North Node

+Pluto/North Node in favorable aspect indicates that the native has strong connections that may be important in achieving his goals. As a transit, it indicates important new connections.

-Pluto/North Node in its unfavorable aspect indicates that the native may suffer through his associations. As a transit, it may indicate a tragic group destiny.

Pluto/Ascendant

+Pluto/Ascendant in its favorable aspect indicates that the native is ambitious and possesses strong will power.

-Pluto/Ascendant in its negative aspect indicates violent arguments, accidents and injuries resulting in a drastic change in the native's life.

Pluto/Midheaven

+Pluto/Midheaven in positive aspect indicates that the native is capable of successfully meeting his goals and obtaining recognition and power.

-Pluto/Midheaven in its negative aspects indicates one who is capable of abusing the power he has obtained. If he does so, he may fall from the heights of success.

QUESTIONNAIRE

1. If you intended to sign a business contract, what aspects would you most prefer?

2. If you intend to purchase or sell a home, what aspects would you prefer?

3. If you have a Jupiter oppose or square Saturn, would you expect a loss or a gain from real estate?

4. If you were to purchase clothing on a Jupiter trine Venus aspect, would you expect to spend a lot of money or find a bargain?

5. What do you think would happen if you violated the law on a Mars Saturn Square or oppose?

6. Would you sign a contract on when Mercury is in its retrograde position?

7. What might you expect under a negative Mars Neptune aspect?

8. What aspect would you choose for a good business trip?

9. What does the sextile offer??

10. What is required under a quincunx?

OTHER CONSIDERATIONS

The Lunation Cycle

Each phase lasts approximately one week.

New Moon

0-45 degrees
The joining of the Sun and the Moon produces an instinctive desire toward creation of an idea.

Crescent Moon

There is an internal struggle due to repeating events and encountering old enemies from this life or a previous lifetime. Old issues must be settled. There is a challenge to let go of the past. Change is necessary for new events.

First Quarter

90-100 degrees
Activities are blocked by people and events in order to force the native onto the correct path. A crisis may be brought about in order to clear the past and usher in the new. This may bring aggressive and impulsive action. It becomes necessary to use one's will in order to manage the crisis.

Gibbous Moon

135-180 degrees
Whatever was started in the new moon phase is near to completion, but more is needed. There is a need to find the pathway for growth and development of the soul.

Full Moon

180-135 degrees
Think before acting or speaking or relationship problems may occur. What was begun at the new moon is now completed. If what was built

has a purpose, it will last. If not, it will more than likely dissipate or breakdown.

Disseminating Moon

135-90 degrees

There is opportunity to expand whatever came into existence at the full moon. It is highly likely that it will be favorably accepted.

Last Quarter

90-45 degrees

The last quarter moon introduces a period of reassessment. It is time to ask what must be done to promote further growth.

Balsamic Moon

45-0 degrees

The black moon is the final phase of the lunation. Plans are drawn; a commitment to a new idea or project emerges, perhaps, ahead of its time.

QUESTIONAIRE

1. What type of problems might occur under a full moon if you do not think before acting or speaking?

2. What is the Black Moon?

3. Describe what may occur under a First Quarter Moon.

Asteroids in the Natal Chart

Many computerized astrological programs have the ability to calculate natal and progressed charts complete with the asteroids, Chiron and the fixed stars. Among the most commonly used asteroids are:

Ceres

Ceres, the Goddess of the Harvest represents the discipline to live together.

Ceres in Aries produces a conflict between the masculine drive and feminine gentleness. Natives are always busy and goal oriented, but may become bored before completion of their projects.

Ceres in Taurus produces a desire to grow gardens or health foods. These natives are good neighbors and are quick to help others.

Ceres in Cancer trains and teaches. Impersonal, they are not cuddlers. There is a practical expression of domesticity that relieves the moodiness of Cancer.

Ceres in Leo offers a love and respect of children and nature. These people may be excellent gardeners, potters, ecology minded, and PTA members.

Ceres in Virgo is a nurturer, interested in nutrition.

Ceres in Libra is fair, honest, reliable, and dependable. These people are interested in equal employment opportunities.

Ceres in Scorpio is goal oriented and ignores setbacks. Naturally psychic, they have strong regenerative powers and recover quickly from illness.

Ceres in Sagittarius is enthusiastic and has a strong sense of freedom. Physically, they often have warts, tumors, and cysts that may need to be removed.

Ceres in Capricorn enjoys learning, is a natural leader, and refuses to accept defeat.

Ceres in Aquarius is tactful, compromises, and is well liked.

Ceres in Pisces is intuitive and will impersonally analyze all experiences.

Pallas

Pallas, The Goddess of Wisdom deals with mental activities in the chart.

Pallas in Aries is inefficient, beginning more projects than he or she can complete. Innovative, they may be pioneers. Mental pressures may cause strain.

Pallas in Taurus is artistic. This placement may produce decorators and designers.

Pallas in Gemini is optimistic, with good mental powers. This position may produce teachers and lecturers.

Pallas in Cancer is the protector of the family and home. He or she may be interested in genealogy and history.

Pallas in Leo possesses self-confidence and is in tune with his environment. The master or mistress of finesse, this native achieves his goals.

Pallas in Virgo is constructive, cheerful, and enjoys serving others.

Pallas in Libra is able to compromise with others but is not able to evaluate objectively.

Pallas in Scorpio is an excellent researcher and has an awareness of human values. He or she is able to see an overview of an issue and discard the frivolous.

Pallas in Sagittarius is positive, confident, and reliable.

Pallas in Capricorn is responsible and evaluates fairly.

Pallas in Aquarius is a humanitarian, enjoys group endeavors, possesses a fine sense of timing, and makes a good astrologer.

Pallas in Pisces enjoys music and people they consider impractical. They often work in hospitals.

Juno

Juno, Goddess of Marriage represents legal marriages.

Juno in Aries searches for a pioneering mate who will be active in public affairs.

Juno in Taurus chooses mates who are reliable and practical.

Juno in Gemini desires a mate who is in reality his or her playmate. One partner often becomes more advanced, either socially or mentally, leaving his or her spouse behind as if he or she were a dependent child.

Juno in Cancer manipulates others. When this native feels he has been treated badly, he will go to any length to seek justice. He or she looks for a spouse who is interested in traditions and will accept the responsibility of home and hearth.

Juno in Leo desires lovers who possess a flair for the dramatic and are willing to share their spotlight. It is difficult for these people to have casual affairs.

Juno in Virgo desires a clean mate, one who is precise and unassuming. They insist upon fairness.

Juno in Libra desires a harmonious, musical, artistic and intelligent spouse. They believing in equal partnerships as well as beauty and balance in the home.

Juno in Scorpio has a strong sense of fairness in concern to obligations. Private, a quiet, but strong spouse appeals to Juno in Scorpio. A warning: This placement has a problem with open communications.

Juno in Sagittarius desires freedom and may be happy with a spouse who introduces travel and new interests into their lives though they may be wed to their career.

Juno in Capricorn is demanding in his or her relationships and expects his or her spouse to work just as hard as he does. They have a deep sense of responsibility and must be appreciated, or they become upset.

Juno in Aquarius either adores his or her mate or seeks subservience from him or her. Juno in this position seeks a free and outspoken mate but may encounter problems with them.

Juno in Pisces maneuvers others. He or she desires a religious mate.

Vesta

Vesta, Goddess of the Hearth

Vesta in Aries desires to improve every situation and will initiate work for humanitarian or spiritual purposes. They will sacrifice for a cause they believe to be important.

Vesta in Taurus possesses intense physical desires and is in conflict between his or her duties and his or her wishes.

Vesta in Gemini is decisive and mentally focused. They may sacrifice for their beliefs. If these people are not mentally compatible with their spouse, the native may become frigid.

Vesta in Cancer possesses a strong responsibility to home and family.

Vesta in Leo may be detached and is able to control his feelings. They are focused upon their own beliefs and may be incapable of considering others.

Vesta in Virgo willingly sacrifices his desires to serve others.

Vesta in Scorpio seems to be constantly judging others. He or she may possess psychic abilities. This placement lends itself to a total regeneration of the personality.

Vesta in Sagittarius is dedicated to religious principles and studies for practical purposes.

Vesta in Capricorn will sacrifice personal fame and fortune for duty and security. If they do not measure up to the demands made upon them, they develop strong guilt complexes.

Vesta in Aquarius is dedicated to carrying out his responsibilities while denying his own personal desires until his task is completed.

Vesta in Pisces sacrifices his personality for his ideals. These people will suffer periods of celibacy for spiritual purposes.

Chiron

Discovered in 1977, Chiron is the bridge to the outer planets of Uranus, Neptune and Pluto. Its orbit is on a fifty to fifty-one year cycle between Saturn and Uranus. It is said to be the gate to the philosopher's stone.

Chiron's position is now included most of our ephemerides. After learning the basics of beginning astrology, I would recommend reading one of the excellent books written on Chiron.

Questionnaire

1.   Name the Asteroids

2.   What does Ceres represent?

3.   What type of activities does Pallas deal with?

FURTHER STUDIES

Fixed Stars

Fixed stars may add much to a natal chart and world events as far as the astrologer is concerned. If nothing else, you will find them fascinating. Originally, the fixed stars were used in atmospheric phenomena. Later, they were used in association with health and illness. A small orb of no more than .30 should be used when fixed stars conjunct other stellar bodies.

Following are a few fixed stars and their brief interpretations. There are a total of seventy-three fixed stars. If you find this study interesting, you may wish to read *Fixed Stars and their Interpretation* by Ebertin-Hoffman, published by the American Federation of Astrologers, Copyright 1971.

Deneb Kaitos, 1 degree 51 minutes Aries (1950) Beta Ceti, magnitude 1

This is located in the Tail of the Whale. Properties: Saturn Associated with this fixed star are inhibitions and restraint, physically and psychologically.

Algol, 25 degrees 28 minutes Taurus, Beta in Perseus

This name is derived from the Arabic *Al Ghoul* interpreted as demon. It is part of a double star system. The dark one has the property of Saturn; the other of Saturn, Mars-Uranus-Pluto.

Example: Mass-murderer Haarmann, Agol is conjunct with his ascendant and in conjunction to Mars. This points to his own nature as a killer and also to his execution.

Another example: Elsbeth Ebertin Her Sun conjuncted Algol and was 2 ½ degrees from Pluto. She was a gentle woman and would not harm a soul. In spite of a warning, she was always in danger and could not avoid the air raid on Freiberg.

Confirmation has been repeated that life offers great handicaps if Saturn and Mars are conjunct with Algol. Strangely enough, in conjunction with this fixed star, artificial teeth are often the case.

Alcyone, 26 degrees nineteen minutes Taurus, Eta Tauri, the main star of the Pleiades

The star's influence is a combination of Moon and Mars. If well connected, it offers ambition, endeavors, honor and glory. But when in aspect to the lights (Sun and Moon) or Mars and Saturn, the eyesight may be affected, or injuries to the eyes may occur.

The Southern Cross, 11 degrees eleven minutes of Scorpio, Alpha and Beta Crucis

The Southern Cross has a Jupiter nature and is quite beneficial if its latitude is the same as the ascendant. It offers intuition, an understanding of the inner nature of others, a preference for the occult, and a religious nature connected with mystical interests.

INTERPRETING THE CHART

"Now what do I do, and where do I start?"

That is exactly what I asked after I had learned the basics. Everyone has their own techniques, but the following is the process I use.

First of all, what are the elements? How many planets are in the water, earth air and fire signs? How many cardinal, fixed and mutable signs are there in the chart? How many masculine and feminine signs are there?

Secondly, read the interpretation of your ascendant. Remember, the ascendant indicates your manner of self-expression, your character, abilities, appearance and your early environment. If there is a planet conjunct with your ascendant, read the interpretation for that planet.

In what house is the ruler of your ascendant placed? If your ascendant is Aries, your ruler is Mars. Read the interpretation for the placement of the ruler.

Are planets placed in your first house? If so, read the interpretation of the planets placed there. For instance, if Venus is in Aries and is placed in your first house, read the interpretation for both Venus in Aries and Venus in the first house.

Next, read the interpretation of your sun sign and the house it is placed in. The sun sign is the way you express your basic energy potential and is your creative drive to grow and develop as an individual. Your sun sign indicates the stage of growth represented by your present incarnation and lessons you must learn.

Follow with the Moon, its sign, and the house it is placed in.

Now, begin with the second house. Where is the ruler located… what sign and house? Are there planets in your second house? If so, read the interpretations.

Continue around the zodiac in the same manner.

Take notes while you're doing this and don't panic if you see something negative.

Now, you may read the aspects formed in your natal chart. Many computerized charts have the aspects as well as interpretations, but not all.

When you're finished and believe you have interpreted your natal or birth chart correctly, you may begin with current transits that will point out trends. One aspect won't mean much, but if you have three aspects pointing to a trend, then it's probably a strong possibility that it is valid. But remember, astrology is not fortune telling; both you and everyone who has ever been born have been given free will by God.

There are several Ephemerides available. I use *The American Ephemeris for the 21st Century* by Neil F. Michelsen, but there are others available. I also take a handy little *Pocket Astrologer* by Jim Maynard with me on trips.

While you're learning the basics and later, when you enter into more advanced astrology, don't panic or become too elated when you are interpreting a chart or an aspect. Analyze everything slowly and carefully. Make certain you've done it correctly.

If you're single and looking ahead for aspects signifying your wedding but there's not an eligible man in sight, don't purchase a bridal gown right away! Those Venus/Jupiter aspects you saw might not be a wedding. You may just take a wonderful vacation, have fun with your sister or a girlfriend, or spend a great deal of money on art or jewelry.

Then again, if you find three aspects pointing to an accident, do be careful. Take out insurance on that rental car if you need to travel. Be more patient than usual. Don't rush out impulsively to the grocery in a blinding rain storm. Remember free will? Use it.

There are many different types of astrology to learn and I guarantee it will be challenging and fun. You don't need to make a career out of it unless you want to. In that case, you will need to learn more advanced techniques.

THE UNITED STATES CHART

4 Jul, 1776 Time: 5:10 PM Philadelphia, Pa USA

There are several dates for the US Chart. This one I found in the "Horoscopes of the U.S. States and Cities" and believe it to be reliable.

When constructing the United States Chart, remember that it must be read or interpreted differently than an individual's natal chart. Following, are the meaning of the houses.

The first house represents the people and the nation.

The second house represents the country's assets.

The third house represents public opinion, communication, transportation and the neighboring countries.

The fourth house represents the land, agriculture and weather. It rules the opposition to the party in power and mining.

The fifth house rules children, education, the birthrate, risks and gambling.

The sixth house represents public health, the armed services, the nature of the illness affecting the people of the country.

The seventh house governs relationships with other nations.

The eighth house represents death and taxes owed to us by foreign countries.

The ninth house represents imports, publishing, the Supreme Court, religion and the clergy. It also represents shipping, trade, science, long-distance travel and inventions.

The tenth house rules the president and the administration.

The eleventh house represents Congress, allies and the wishes of the country.

The twelfth house represents pensions, hospitals and crime or criminals.

BIRTHDATES OF FAMOUS PEOPLE

Following are birthdates of a few famous people. Their birthdate information was obtained from the Janus 3.0 Astrology program. You may find it interesting to construct their charts for research purposes.

George Walker Bush - Date: 6 July Time: 7:26 AM EDT Place: New Haven, Ct. USA

Bill Clinton - Date: 19 Aug 1946 Time: 8:51 AM CST Hope, Arkansas USA

Madonna - Date: 16 Aug 1958 Time: 7:00 AM EST Bay City, MI USA

Marilyn Monroe - Date: 1 Jun 1926 Time: 9:30 AM PST Los Angeles, Ca, USA

Picasso - Date: 25 Oct 1881 Time: 11:15 PM Malaga, Spain

Leonardo da Vince – Date: 23 Apr 1452 9:40 PM Vinci, Italy

Mozart – Date: 27 Jan, 1756 Time: 8:00 PM Salzburg, Austria

Glossary

afflicted - A planet is referred to as afflicted when it is poorly aspected; when in square, opposition, conjunction or quincunx to other planets or an angular cusp.

angles - The four points of the chart sectioning it into quadrants.

ascendant - The cusp of the first house or the eastern horizon is referred to as the ascendant.

arc - The "arc" in astrological terms is the zodiacal longitude.

asteroids - The asteroids are occasionally used by astrologers and are sometimes placed on the natal chart in a computerized horoscope. They are planetoids; small celestial bodies whose orbits are placed between Mars and Jupiter. The major ones are Ceres, Pallas, Juno and Vesta.

composite chart - A composite chart is a chart using midpoints between pairs of planets in two or more horoscopes to be interpreted as a relationship chart.

decant - A decant is a ten-degree segment of a sign.

descendant - The descendant is the opposite angle from the rising sign that describes the native's partner.

detriment - The sign of a planet's detriment is always opposite to the sign of its rulership and is at its weakest when it is in its detriment.

durinal - A durinal is the opposite of nocturnal.

exaltation - A planet is said to be in its exaltation when it is favorably placed in a sign. For example, Sun in Aries; Moon in Taurus; Mercury in Virgo; Venus in Pisces; Mars in Capricorn; Jupiter in Cancer; Saturn in Libra; Uranus in Scorpio; Neptune in Cancer; Pluto in Pisces

fall - A planet is said to be in its fall when it is unfavorably placed. This position is always opposite of its exhaltation position.

glyph - A glyph is the symbol for an astrological sign.

Electional Astrology - Horary astrology is sometimes referred to as Electional astrology. It deals with the selecting a specific time for an event to take place.

elements - The elements are fire, earth, air and water.

exaltations - The planets are at their strongest in the sign which they rule are in their rulership or exaltation.

feminine signs - Taurus, Cancer, Virgo, Scorpio, Capricorn and Pisces are the feminine signs or the most receptive in the zodiac.

Greenwich Mean Time GMT is universal time...the time at the prime meridian. It is the standard time used for navigation, astronomy and astrology.

Horary Astrology - Horary astrology is a branch of astrology calculated at a specific time the question is asked in order to receive an accurate answer.

Immum Coeli - The Immum Coeli is the Nadir...the opposite point of the Mid-heaven in the natal chart or the cusp of the Fourth House. It is also the northern point of the chart.

ingress - Ingess is the entrance of a planet into a sign.

inner planets - The inner planets are the faster moving planets...the Sun, Moon, Mercury, Venus and Mars.

intercepted Signs - Intercepted signs never occur in the zodiac. They occur in horoscopes when a sign appears to be in a house, but not on a house cusp.

luminaries - The luminaries are the lights; the Sun and the Moon.

malefics - Saturn is said to be the greater malefic while Mars is considered to be the lesser of the negative or evil planets. Actually, there are no evil planets or signs. They may form negative aspects within a horoscope, but the planets themselves or signs are not evil.

masculine Signs - The masculine signs possessing the most aggressive energy are Gemini, Leo, Libra, Sagittarius and Aquarius.

midheaven or the cusp of the tenth House. It is also referred to as the MC or the Medium Coeli.

midpoint - The mid-point is the point equally distant between two planets.

stationary - The position in which a planet appears to be motionless just before or after a planet goes into its retrograde or direct position.

void of course - A planet is said to be Void of Course when it will form no further aspects before it enters the next zodiac sign.

Bibliography

"Romancing The Zodiac" by Wes Alistair
Published by 1stbooks Library Copyright 1999

"The Essence" by William Brock Published by Brockhouse
Publishing, Naples, Fl. 1998

"Chiron" by Barbara Hand Clow

"Astroids in the Birth Chart" by Emma Belle Donath

"The Combination of Stellar Influences" by Reinhold Ebertin
Published by the American Federation of Astrologers, most recent
copyright 1972

"Fixed Stars and their Interpretation" by Ebertin-Hoffman

"The New A to Z" by Llewellyn George, Revised and Edited by
Marylee Bytheriver
Published by Llewellyn Publications 1990

"A Spiritual Approach To Astrology" by Myrna Lofthus published
by CRCS Publications copyright 1983

Predictive Astrology' by Francis Sakoian & Louis Acker published
by Harper & Roe

"The Astrologer's Handbook" by Fransces Sakoian & Louise S. Acker
Published by Harper & Roe, Publishers copyright 1973

"Horoscopes of the U.S. States and Cities"

Wikopedia

About The Author

Wes Alistair, pseudonym for Weslynn McCallister, is a writer, a poet and an astrologer, specializing in astrological research. A member of the American Federation of Astrologers, she has been studying astrology for over twenty-five years. After "Romancing the Zodiac" was published, she wrote a monthly column in "The Light," published out of Albuquerque, New Mexico. Her astrological poems have been published in the AFA bulletins as well as on her web site that also includes notes of astrological interest such as retrogrades, meteorites, comets and eclipse dates.

She lives in Southwest Florida. When she's not busy writing, she enjoys traveling, dancing, and attending live musical performances and plays. Taking long walks on half-way deserted beaches is also a favorite pastime. Her website is: http://www.weslynn.com